A PHARMACY LAW REVIEW

MPJE

Texas

Editors

Anthony J. Busti, MD, PharmD, MSc, FNLA, FAHA
Craig Cocchio, PharmD, BCPS, DABAT
Cassie Boland, PharmD, BCACP, CDCES
Donnie Nuzum, PharmD, BCACP, BC-ADM, CDCES
P. Brittany Vickery, PharmD, BCPS, BCPP

MPJE Texas: A Pharmacy Law Review (2nd Edition)

Published in the United States of America by High-Yield Med Reviews
P.O. Box 690044 | San Antonio, TX 78269
www.highyieldmedreviews.com

High-Yield Med Reviews is an official brand of MedEducation, LLC. MedEducation, LLC does business as (dba) High-Yield Med Reviews. High-Yield Med Reviews is a registered trademark of MedEducation, LLC in the United States of America.

ISBN 979-8-8652595-4-1

HIGH-YIELD
MED REVIEWS

Helpful Study Tip
Please Read

This Rapid Review is based on the NABP MPJE Competency Statements which summarize the topics covered on the exam. The Competency Statements provide an *outline* to aid in preparation for the exam, however this review also includes additional key elements in the laws that are essential to know when preparing for the state MPJE.

- The NABP MPJE Competency Statements do NOT include all exam content.
- No distinction is made between federal and state jurisprudence questions on the MPJE. You must answer each question based on the state's prevailing laws where you seek licensure.
- The best preparation for the MPJE combines formal education, training, practical experience, and self-study.
- Additional information may also be obtained from the licensing state board of pharmacy.

If you have not done so yet, we recommend you watch our short video on how to study for the MPJE using our program.

SCAN ME

Need help with the NAPLEX exam?

High-Yield Med Review's
Study Tools for the NAPLEX

Lectures & Books

- Reflects content tested
- 240+ topics available
- Organized by topic areas
- HD lectures for quality
- Works on all devices
- Monitors your progress

Q-Bank

- 2,000+ practice questions
- Select topic categories
- Teaching points provided
- Performance statistics
- Ability to flag questions
- Peer comparison metrics

Live Reviews

- Live, in-person events
- Live stream events
- Study with your peers
- Taught by expert faculty

Practice Exam

- 150 question exam
- Delivered on computer
- Build test taking skills
- Gain endurance
- Assess your level of preparation

Rapid Review

- Review core concepts quickly.
  - NAPLEX Rapid Review Book
  - NAPLEX Rapid Review Webinar Series
- Final step in comprehensive review

Other Study Tools

- MPJE Exam - Law Review
- Top 300 Drugs Review
- Other tools available :
  - Top 65 Acute Care Drugs
  - Top 50 OTC Drug Review
  - Top 25 Herbals Review
  - Landmark Clinical Trials Reviews

Want to upgrade at a discount?

Need help or a study plan?

We can help!
Contact us for a discount to upgrade to our premium package for the tools you need to prepare and pass.
customerservice@highyieldmedreviews.com

Table of Contents

PHARMACY PRACTICE for MPJE (CONT'D)

STATE SPECIFIC REVIEW ALIGNED BY NABP

STATE SPECIFIC - PHARMACY PRACTICE   103

High-Yield Med Reviews

M P J E
Review Course

Successful Preparation Strategies

To win any game, you have to understand the rules. Taking an exam is no different. If you understand what it takes to pass, you can use that to your advantage to study more efficiently and effectively. Don't waste your time and efforts by skipping this section!

How to Successfully Study for the MPJE

Watch this short video that teaches you how to study for the MPJE using our program

High-Yield Med Review's
4 Steps for SUCCESS on the MPJE Exam

 1   **B E F O R E   T H E   E X A M**

- **ORIENT YOURSELF**
    - The MPJE assesses your ability to apply the laws and regulations for a specific North American state/jurisdiction to pharmacy practice. You must pass the MPJE for each state/jurisdiction in which you want to practice pharmacy.
    - Eligibility, requirements, and timelines vary between jurisdictions. Be sure to check with your pharmacy board for more details: https://nabp.pharmacy/about/boards-of-pharmacy/

    Watch our video tutorials to ensure you are studying correctly:

    Watch this first →

    SCAN ME

- **KEEP THE RIGHT MINDSET**
It's a well-known fact: Studying the law is challenging and dry (i.e., boring) for most people who are taking the MPJE. Unfortunately, it tends to be comprised mostly of simple memorization. We have tried to summarize the most important parts of the publicly available law in a bullet point format to help you with this. BUT, don't forget to keep the right mindset throughout your studies: You don't just need to know the facts, you need to be ready to *apply* them to clinical scenarios. As you memorize the points, consider how they might be used in your future practice.

- **STUDY ACCURATELY**
    - The MPJE is focused on *state-specific law* that is in the *context of the federal law*: Meaning some states do not fill in all gaps, which is where the federal law takes effect. If a topic is not covered in the state portion of this book, it was NOT an accident. In these cases, you must defer to the federal laws to guide you.
    - Focus your studying on well-established topics and concepts.
    - NOTE: Actual calculations are not likely to be tested on the MPJE, but you still need to understand their core concepts in order to compound and/or fill a legal prescription.

- **PRACTICE**
Get your mind in the game, and **practice**! You may know the laws, but if you aren't prepared to express that in a 120-question multiple-choice format, you will likely struggle on this exam. To combat this common error, we offer an MPJE Q-Bank. Practicing is one of the best ways to ensure success.

Get the Q-bank here →
If you purchased this product through a retailer, you are eligible for a discounted upgrade to the Q-bank package!

 SCAN ME

High-Yield Med Review's
4 Steps for SUCCESS on the MPJE Exam

 2 **MORNING OF THE EXAM**

- **STOP STUDYING**

    Stop studying the night before the exam and do something fun. Relax and go to sleep early. Your brain will continue to process the information you've studied and make subconscious connections while you are NOT consciously studying – give it the chance to do so!

- **BREAKFAST**

    You need to eat breakfast, but you should avoid high carbs (simple sugars) and high fats that can lead to post-prandial fatigue and steal blood flow from your brain to your gut! Good options for breakfast:
    - Complex carbs such as fresh fruits and vegetables
    - Quality proteins for *sustained energy* without brain steal: fish, lean bacon, eggs.
    - Adequate hydration but NOT excessive fluids

- **ARRIVE EARLY**
    - Arrive 30 minutes before your scheduled time to complete check in. If you are more than 30 minutes late, you will be required to start the process over (including fees).
    - Bring ID: US or Canadian Passport, Driver's License, State/Military/Temporary ID
      *Tip: Ensure they are not expired, and that they match the exact name you used on both your transcript and your NABP e-profile when registering for the exam.

- **KNOW WHAT TO EXPECT**
    - You will be given materials to do scratch work on.
    - Your entire exam will take place on a computer, so consider bringing what you might need to remain comfortable and focused, such as blue-light filtering glasses.
    - Breaks will not be scheduled during this exam. You may retreat to a break room at any time for snacks, drinks, restroom use, etc; however, your exam clock will continue to run.

High-Yield Med Review's
4 Steps for SUCCESS on the MPJE Exam

3	DURING THE EXAM

- **PACE YOURSELF**
  You have 2.5 hours to complete 120 questions, so an average of 1.5 minutes per question. That said, be careful not to speed through unreasonably as you cannot go back to previous questions.

- **STAY ORIENTED**
  Answer questions according to how they fit the state law first; when the state law doesn't guide you to the correct answer, defer to federal law.

- **ANSWER ALL QUESTIONS!**
  Do NOT leave any question unanswered. You must answer a minimum of 107 questions, and any left unanswered after that will be considered incorrect. Statistically, you are better off blindly guessing than leaving anything blank.

- **ELIMINATE**
  Eliminate answer choices with extreme wording (e.g., never, always, etc.), as they are often wrong.

- **AVOID THE NERVES AND NEGATIVE THOUGHTS**
  MOST people feel they are going to fail the MPJE exam, but in fact end up passing. The questions can seem confusing or different from what you think you studied – that is common, so do not let it frustrate you. Keep your mind in the game.

- **ASK YOURSELF**
  - "What is the core concept being tested here?" This often reveals the correct choice.
  - "How does this fit the context of the state-specific law?"
  - If you find two possible right answers, ask yourself what is wrong with each one to find the "better" or "more accurate" answer for this particular question.
  - If you are stuck or running out of time, choose answer "C" (which is statistically the more common correct answer choice), take a breath, and move on.

High-Yield Med Review's

4 Steps for SUCCESS on the MPJE Exam

4 | **AFTER THE EXAM**

- **IF YOU FEEL GREAT**
  You probably did great: Celebrate!! You are a huge step closer to practicing pharmacy.

- **IF YOU FEEL LOUSY**
  DO NOT STRESS!
    - A large majority of pharmacists report feeling this way after taking their MPJE. It is a common feeling, and it tends to be inaccurate. While most people feel this way, they in fact end up passing. As such, there is no sense in getting frustrated or upset until you receive your score.
    - If you are having a hard time letting go of these feelings, try using them productively by taking some notes for yourself while you are still in the test-taking mindset. For example, note what topic areas gave you trouble; or if you had a hard time remembering a certain law, notate it now so that you can easily return to it in the future if needed.

- **RELAX**
  Regardless, take a moment to relax now. No matter your results, you are now one step closer to actually practicing pharmacy. Even if you do have to retake your MPJE, you now have invaluable experience under your belt.

- **RESULTS**
    - The timeline for receiving your score varies depending on your jurisdiction. Many will be accessible within 14 days of the exam; however, you should check with your pharmacy board for specifics.
    - Results will be pass/fail. If you fail, you will be given a general idea of how weak or strong you were according to each competency statement.
    - Once you get your score, please let us know how you did and/or if there is anything we can do better to serve you and the profession of pharmacy. We genuinely care how we are serving the profession, and value both good and bad feedback.

Helpful Note
Please Read

A Note About
Calculations

The NABP does not explicitly state whether or not calculations will be on the MPJE exam in the most current competency statements. Historically, a basic knowledge of core calculations' concepts was necessary in order for a pharmacist to properly apply certain aspects of the law; this typically centered around compounding and/or properly dispensing a legal prescription order.

As such, we have chosen to include some of these core concepts related to calculations for those who feel they need this additional information where applicable to that state since this specific topic can vary from one state to another.

If you have not done so yet, PLEASE watch this short video on how to study for the MPJE using our program. It WILL help you.

SCAN ME

MPJE
Q-BANK

SCAN ME

Did you miss the Q-bank?

If you purchased this product through a retailer, and you didn't get the Q-bank package, it's not too late! Scan the QR code above to gain discounted access to these vital MPJE Practice Questions.

————————

"You can't expect to pass your exam just by reading a book or listening to a lecture; you must PRACTICE what you are being asked to do."

- Anthony J. Busti, MD, PharmD, MSc, FNLA, FAHA

"Memorizing the laws is straightforward, but interpreting them gets fuzzy very quickly, and everyone struggles with APPLYING them to scenarios and test questions. Students who don't practice this aspect usually walk out of the exam feeling like they've failed. Don't let that happen to you."

- Cassie Boland, PharmD, BCACP, CDCES

M P J E
Review Course

Federal & General Topic Reviews

If you have not yet done so, PLEASE watch this short video on how to study for the MPJE using our program. It WILL help you.

SCAN ME

M P J E

Review Course

Federal & General Topic Reviews

Federal Law

FEDERAL LAW & REGULATIONS – REGULATORY AGENCIES

The U.S. healthcare system has several regulatory bodies formed by federal laws intended to improve the safety and quality of services to the public.

Healthcare organizations and participants providing healthcare-related services must comply with and ensure standards are met to operate and receive funding.

Overview of Regulatory Bodies

- **Food & Drug Administration (FDA)**
  (21 US Code. § 301, 353, 355; 21 CFR § 314.92)

  - **Pure Food and Drug Act (1906)**
    - Prohibited interstate commerce of misbranded and adulterated foods, drinks, and drugs.
    - Defined misbranding and adulteration.

  - **Harrison Narcotics Tax Act (1914)**
    - Regulated and taxed production, importation, distribution, and use of opiates or cocaine.

  - **Food, Drug, and Cosmetic Act (1938)**
    - Enforced by the FDA
    - Also implements the Drug Quality and Security Act (DQSA) which includes:
      - The Compounding Quality Act that defines outsourcing compounders and creates a voluntary registration program.
      - The Drug Supply Chain Security Act (DSCSA) that helps track products throughout distribution using a nationally electronic system.
    - Drugs are recognized by the USP/NF or Homeopathic Pharmacopeia as intended for diagnosis, cure, mitigation, treatment, or prevention of diseases, not food.
      - Dietary supplements (considered food) and cosmetics are not considered drugs.

  - **Durham-Humphrey Amendments (1951)**
    - Required specific drugs to be available through a prescription only.
      - A prescription drug is defined as one that is unsafe for self-medication and can only be used under a prescriber's supervision.
      - Also, established OTC drugs can be purchased without a prescription.
    - Any drug possessing a habit-forming property or that is potentially harmful must have the following on the label: "Caution: Federal law prohibits dispensing without a prescription."

  - **Kefauver-Harris Amendment (1962)**
    - Thalidomide taken by pregnant women to relieve morning sickness, which is one indication among others, causes congenital malformations (phocomelia).
    - Reviewed by Francis Kelsey at the FDA, where it was denied approval in the U.S.
    - Prompted development of this amendment that updated the new drug approval process.
    - Evaluation of safety and efficacy of new drug products pending approval requires a 3-step process.
      - Step 1 – In vivo animal studies
      - Step 2 – Submission of Investigational New Drug (IND) application
      - Step 3 – Clinical trials
        - Phase 1 – Assesses toxicologic, pharmacokinetic, and pharmacologic properties of a drug in healthy humans
        - Phase 2 – A larger group than phase 1 with disease targeted by a new drug

- Phase 3 – Larger group study for drug safety and efficacy compared to placebo or established control
- Step 4 – New Drug Application Process
  - Phase 4 – Postmarketing research
  - MedWatch allows adverse event reporting by healthcare practitioners to the FDA or manufacturer.

- **Comprehensive Drug Abuse Prevention and Control Act (1970)**
  - Provides the classification, acquisition, distribution, registration/verification of prescribers, and appropriate record-keeping requirements of controlled substances.
  - Established the Drug Enforcement Administration (DEA)

- **Poison Prevention Packaging Act (1970)**
  - Gave the Consumer Product Safety Commission (CPSC) authority to mandate child-safe special packaging of products and drugs to protect children from harm.
  - This packaging should be difficult for children under 5 to open to provide enough time for the parent or guardian to notice the child trying to open it.

- **Medical Device Amendments (1976)**
  - Brought guidance on devices (ranging from tongue depressors to intrauterine devices) similar to drugs.

- **Federal Antitampering Act (1983)**
  - Cyanide was made into tablets identical to acetaminophen tablets and put into bottles bought by many in the Chicago area. Unfortunately, the ingestion of single tablets led to the death of several individuals, prompting urgent warnings.
  - This event resulted in the requirement for tamper-evident bottles and devices.

- **Orphan Drug Act (1983)**
  - Diseases affecting fewer than 200,000 people in the U.S. or less than 5 people per 10,000 in a community can be evaluated under the Orphan Drug Act.
  - This Act reduces the requirement for research and development of drugs for these diseases.
  - In addition, it extends the time of market exclusivity for 7 years post-approval and provides tax reductions during this time.

- **Drug Price Competition and Patent-Term Restoration Act (Hatch-Waxman Act) (1984)**
  - Amendment to the FDC Act developed so that marketers of generic drugs can file an Abbreviated New Drug Application for FDA generic approval.
  - Provides an accelerated path to market for low-cost generics.

- **Prescription Drug Marketing Act (1987)**
  - Addressed prescription drug-marketing practices that contributed to the diversion of large quantities of drugs to a secondary gray market which established a drug diversion market.
  - Prohibits the act or offer of knowingly selling, purchasing, or trading a prescription drug sample.
  - Prohibits the resale of any prescription drug previously purchased by a hospital or other healthcare entity.

- **Omnibus Budget Reconciliation Act (1987) (OBRA-87)**
  - Federal Nursing Home Reform Act was established to protect patients' rights in long-term care facilities.
  - Provided the Centers for Medicare and Medicaid Services (CMS) authority to develop measures that reduce unnecessary costs while improving the quality of patient care.

- **Anabolic Steroids Control Act (1990)**
    - Moved anabolic steroids to Schedule III controlled substances to reduce their use for non-medical purposes.

- **Omnibus Budget Reconciliation Act (1990) (OBRA-90)**
    - Sought to improve therapeutic outcomes by imposing pharmacist counseling obligations, prospective drug utilization review, and record-keeping mandates.
    - Elevated the expectations of pharmacists' interaction with patients.
    - Drug utilization reviews require pharmacists to review:
        - Therapeutic duplication
        - Incorrect drug dosage
        - Incorrect duration of treatment
        - Drug-disease contraindications
        - Drug-drug interactions
        - Drug-allergy interactions
        - Clinical abuse/misuse of medication

    - Information the pharmacist is to discuss with the patient during counseling
        - Name and description of the medicine
        - Dosage form, dosage, administration route, and drug therapy duration
        - Common severe adverse effects, interactions, and therapeutic contraindications
        - Techniques for self-monitoring of drug therapy
        - Particular directions and the patient's cautions for preparation and administration
        - Proper storage
        - Refill information
        - Action to be taken in the event of a missed dose

- **Dietary Supplement Health and Education Act (1994)**
    - Defined dietary supplements as a product intended to supplement the diet and has one or more of the following:
        - Amino acid
        - Mineral
        - Herb
        - Vitamin
        - Dietary substances to supplement the diet by increasing the total dietary intake
        - Concentrate, metabolite, constituent, extract, or combination of any of the above

- **Health Insurance Portability and Accountability Act (1996) (HIPAA)**
    - Designed to safeguard the privacy of protected health information.

- **Food and Drug Administration Modernization Act (1997)**
    - Sought the regulation of foods, drugs, devices, and biological products characterized by increasing technological, trade, and public health complexities.

- **Best Pharmaceuticals for Children Act (2002)**
    - Established a two-tiered approach to ensure research of drugs used by pediatric populations.

- **Medicare Modernization Act (2003) (Medicare Part D)**
    - Provides prescription drug coverage to patients eligible for Medicare benefits.
    - Developed medication therapy management services (MTM) where pharmacists can provide and get reimbursed for evaluating a patient's medication profile.

- **Combat Methamphetamine Epidemic Act (2005)**
  - Requires OTC sale of pseudoephedrine to be behind the counter.

- **Medicaid Tamper-Resistant Prescription Law (2007)**
  - Requires electronic or tamper-resistant prescription pads for Medicaid patients.

- **Drug Enforcement Administration (DEA):**

  - Enforces federal laws related to the Controlled Substances Act (CSA).
  - Pertains to manufacturing, distribution, and dispensing of legal products.
  - Investigates and prepares prosecution of activities that violate the CSA.

- **Occupational Safety and Health Administration (OSHA):**

  - Formed from the Occupational Safety and Health Act of 1970
  - Ensures working environment and conditions are safe by setting the standards and assessing compliance.
  - Conducts periodic work site inspections.

- **National Institute for Occupational Safety & Health (NIOSH):**

  - Responsible for "conducting research" and making recommendations for the "prevention" of work-related injury and illness.
  - Comes from the same legislation as OSHA.

- **Centers for Disease Control and Prevention (CDC):**

  - This is the U.S. health protection agency whose purpose is to save lives and protect people from health, safety, and security threats within the U.S. and abroad.
  - Examples include guidelines on infection control, hand-hygiene, standard or universal precautions, and safe injection practices.

Other Standards – USP

- **United States Pharmacopeia (USP):**

  - A non-governmental organization
  - Sets standards for drugs, dietary supplements, and other healthcare products.
    - Published in the United States Pharmacopeia and National Formulary (USP NF)
      - For example, USP Chapter 795 sets standards for nonsterile compounding, USP Chapter 797 sets standards for pharmaceutical compounding of sterile products, and USP Chapter 800 sets standards for handling hazardous drugs.
  - Goals:
    - Advance public health by ensuring the quality of medications, ingredients in foods, and other products
    - Promote safe and proper use of medications
    - Verifying ingredients in dietary supplements

> **⟋⟍ Accelerate Your Knowledge**
>
> ✓ *USP Chapters 795, 797, 800, and 825 are further outlined in their own chapters in this book.*
> ✓ *USP is not a set of laws but is used by legal sources as a standard of practice.*

FEDERAL LAW & REGULATIONS – MEDICARE & MEDICAID PROGRAMS

- **General Background Information**

    - Medicare and Medicaid are the two major healthcare coverage programs in the U.S., supervised by the Centers for Medicare and Medicaid Services (CMS).
        - Medicare is regulated and controlled by the federal government.
        - Medicaid has some federal government oversight but is regulated mostly by the states.
    - The Medicare Prescription Drug Improvements and Modernization Act (MMA) created 4 programs in Medicare named Parts A-D.

Part	Purpose
A	Provides insurance for hospitalization
B	Provides insurance for physician services
C	Medicare managed care or Medicare Advantage
D	Provides prescription coverage for drugs

- **Medicare Part D**

    - Medicare patients can enroll in a prescription drug plan (PDP).
        - Medicare contracts with private insurance companies that provide drug-only coverage, or coverage is offered through the Medicare Advantage local plans.
        - Policies apply to individuals, so married couples must each have their own.
        - The cost is income dependent.
            - Patients who are not low-income may pay a monthly premium, annual deductible, and/or co-payments like regular insurance.
        - Co-payments are tier-based.
            - Tier 1 = Lease expensive generic drug
            - Tier 2 = Preferred brand name drug
            - Tier 3 = Non-preferred brand name drug
            - Tier 4 = Rare, high-cost drugs

- **Medicare Formulary Requirements**

    - All standard plans must include options within all USP therapeutic categories.
    - Developed by a P&T Committee that is made up of physicians and pharmacists.
    - Formularies are not required to have all drug options within every class, but for certain classes, most options must be included, such as:
        - Anticonvulsants, antidepressants, antineoplastics, antipsychotics, antiretrovirals, and immunosuppressants

- **Additional features of the Medicare program include:**

    - All prescription benefit programs must accept participation from any pharmacy agreeing to their drug plan.
    - Plans cannot force the patient to obtain drugs through mail-order pharmacies.
    - 90-day supplies for chronic medications are allowed.
    - If a brand-name drug is dispensed, the patient must be informed of the availability of lower-cost options.

- Pharmacists are eligible to get paid for providing medication therapy management (MTM) services for patients enrolled in Part D.
- Drug plans must establish MTM programs for patients to enroll in, especially those with chronic, expensive drugs.
- Allow generic drug companies of a product to have 180 days of exclusivity if they file on the first day of eligibility

FEDERAL LAW & REGULATIONS – FEDERAL FOOD, DRUG AND COSMETIC ACT

Federal Food, Drug, and Cosmetic Act (FD&C Act)
(21 U.S. Code § 331[a])

- **Prohibits introduction or delivery for introduction into interstate commerce of products that are adulterated or misbranded.**

    - This can extend to foods, devices, or cosmetics.
    - Interstate commerce is exchanging the product for money or services between any state, territory, or the District of Columbia.

- **A general description of adulterated or misbranded drugs describes the alteration, mutilation, destruction, obliteration, or removal of the whole or any part of the labeling if these are done when the product is for sale in interstate commerce and causes product adulteration or misbranding.**

Adulterated Drugs (FFDCA)
(21 U.S. Code § 351)

- **Adulteration is further defined in detail within the U.S. Code § 351.**

    - A drug is considered adulterated under numerous criteria, mainly when the drug is, in whole or part, any filthy, putrid, or decomposed substance.
    - There is a failure of a drug or device to satisfy FDA purity standards.
    - Prepared, packed, or held under unsanitary conditions
        - Defined as a drug being exposed to and contaminated with filth or if the drug was determined to be harmful to health from these circumstances.
    - The facility that controls or is used for manufacturing and packaging violates the current good manufacturing practices.
    - The container or storage of the drug is made from anything that can be poisonous or harmful, ultimately causing injury to health.
    - Uses an unsafe color additive for purposes of coloring only.
    - The drug labeling contains all the required fields but incorrectly lists the strength, quantity, or purity outside compendium standards.
    - The drug itself is not listed in an official compendium (such as USP), and its strength differs from, or its quality and purity fall below, what is represented on the label.
    - Any substance has been mixed with the drug to reduce the drug's strength, or any substance has been substituted for the drug.

> ⚖️ **Law Pearl**
>
> ✓ *One illegal adulteration example includes utilizing adulterants in cocaine. Caffeine, diltiazem, hydroxyzine, levamisole, and phenacetin have been used historically in illicit cocaine supplies to mimic its effects yet increase its supply and demand. Levamisole is a notorious cocaine adulterant that was associated with agranulocytosis (causing US market withdrawal), and multifocal inflammatory leukoencephalopathy.*

Misbranded Drugs and Devices

(21 U.S. Code § 352)

- **Misbranding criteria:**
  - The labeling and/or container is false or misleading in any manner.
    - Labeling may refer to any graphic, printed, or written material on any container, the container's wrapper, and any other content accompanying the product.
      - Examples of labels include package inserts, information in tertiary references, and marketing and promotion materials.

> **Accelerate Your Knowledge**
>
> ✓ *Example: A Phase 3 clinical study funded by the drug company demonstrates an improvement in reduction of major cardiac events. However, a healthcare economic analysis done by a formulary committee (or other similar entity with knowledge and expertise in healthcare economic analysis) determines their conclusion differs from the data. The healthcare system opts to decline the addition of this drug to their formulary.*

  - The medication does not bear a label containing the name and place of business of the manufacturer, packer, or distributor and an accurate statement of the quantity of the contents in terms of weight, measure, or numerical count.
    - This also applies to non-prescription drugs (21 U.S. Code § 379aa). In addition, non-prescription drug labels must have a domestic address and phone number where the person who purchased them can report serious adverse events.
  - Incorrectly provides the quantity of the contents in terms of weight, measure, or numerical count.
  - The required information (listed above) is not prominently displayed compared to other wording.
  - The label lacks appropriate directions for use or warnings against use in certain pathological conditions, by children, or against unsafe dosing methods, or duration of administration or application.
    - An exception occurs when the medication is exempt from or fails to have the information required by the NDA.
  - It is dangerous to a person's health when used in the dosage or manner or with the frequency or duration prescribed, recommended, or suggested in the labeling.
  - The labeling fails to identify the name and proportion of the habit-forming substance and, in juxtaposition to that, the phrase "Warning—May be habit-forming."
  - Falls out of compliance regarding color additives (FFDCA Section 706).
  - The medication's name in an official compendium (i.e., USP), or any common or usual name, is not prominently printed in type at least half as large as that used for any proprietary name.
  - The drug is at risk for deterioration, and the labeling does not contain warnings.

> **Fast Facts**
>
> ✓ *A drug can be misbranded if additional risk mitigation is not followed for a drug. One example is olanzapine (Zyprexa Relprevv) long-acting injectable, which has a risk evaluation and mitigation strategy (REMS) program. When pharmacies fail to comply with this REMS program for risk labeling on the prescription communication to prescribers, patients, or others, it is considered misbranded.*

FEDERAL LAW & REGULATIONS – CONTROLLED SUBSTANCES

The CSA sets the rules for prescription products and their scheduling via the Attorney General and DEA.

The level of risk for abuse and physical and/or psychological dependence influences the schedule designation of the product.

Background Information

- **Controlled Substance:**

    - A drug or substance included in Schedule I, II, III, IV, or V of the Controlled Substances Act (CSA)
    - Does not include alcohol-based beverages or tobacco

- **Classification of medications per the Controlled Substance Act (CSA):**

    - Enforced by the Drug Enforcement Administration (DEA)
    - The DEA is under the supervision of the US Attorney General.

- **Controlled Substance Possession and Handling**

    - Researchers, manufacturers, distributors, labs, exporters, narcotic treatment programs, and pharmacies registered with the DEA may possess and handle controlled substances.

    - Must complete appropriate forms:
        - Pharmacies = Form 224
        - Manufacturers, distributors, importers/exporters, or researchers = Form 225
        - Narcotic treatment programs = Form 363

    - A DEA registration is good for 36 months
        - Renewals are sent to registrants 60 days before the expiration date.
        - Note: Pharmacists working at a pharmacy with a DEA license do not have to register with the DEA themselves.

Controlled Substance Designations

- **Schedule I Substances:**

    - High risk of abuse
    - No currently accepted medical use in treating a condition within the US
    - Do not have accepted information related to the safety of their use.
    - Can only be purchased using a DEA 222 form.
    - Examples:
        - Diethylamide
        - Heroin
        - LSD
        - Mescaline
        - Methaqualone
        - Peyote
        - Note: marijuana, but this is likely to change

- **Schedule II Substances:**

    - High potential for abuse and dependence
    - Have currently accepted uses in the US but are under tight restrictions
    - Can only be purchased with a DEA Form 222
    - Examples:
        - Amphetamine
        - Cocaine
        - Codeine
        - Diphenoxylate
        - Fentanyl
        - Hydrocodone
        - Hydromorphone
        - Methadone
        - Methamphetamine
        - Methylphenidate
        - Oxycodone
        - Pentobarbital
        - PCP

- **Schedule III Substances:**

    - Have potential for abuse and dependence but less than schedule II substances
    - Have currently accepted uses in the US.
    - Examples:
        - Acetaminophen + codeine
        - Anabolic steroids (Schedule II in some states)
        - Buprenorphine
        - Butalbital
        - Dronabinol
        - Any compound or formulation containing amobarbital, secobarbital, pentobarbital

- **Schedule IV Substances:**

    - Have a low potential for abuse compared to Schedule III substances.
    - Have currently accepted uses in the US.

- Limited risk of physical or mental dependence compared to Schedule I-III substances.
- Examples:
    - Benzodiazepines
    - Butorphanol
    - Carisoprodol
    - Chlordiazepoxide
    - Eszopiclone
    - Meprobamate
    - Modafinil
    - Pentazocine
    - Phentermine
    - Tramadol
    - Triazolam
    - Zaleplon
    - Zolpidem

- **Schedule V Substances:**

    - Have a low potential for abuse compared to Schedule IV substances.
    - Have currently accepted uses in the US.
    - Limited risk of physical or mental dependence compared to lower schedules
    - Examples:
        - Acetaminophen + codeine elixir
        - Promethazine + codeine
        - Diphenoxylate + atropine
        - Lacosamide
        - Pregabalin

Labeling and Controlled Substances

- **All labels for controlled substances must include the following in addition to normal labeling:**
  "Caution: Federal law prohibits the transfer of this drug to anyone other than the patient for whom it was prescribed."

Purchasing

- **The purchasing of Schedule I & II substances:**

    - Must use DEA Form 222
    - 3 Copies:
        - Copy 1 (Brown) = Goes to the supplier
        - Copy 2 (Green) = First goes to the supplier, which is then forwarded to the DEA
        - Copy 3 (Blue) = Kept by the purchaser
    - Controlled Substances Ordering System (CSOS):
        - Electronic ordering that is faster and more accurate, decreases costs, and allows ordering freedom.

Inventory

- **General requirements**
  (21 CFR 1304.11)

  - Biennial inventory (at least every 2 years)
  - Complete an accurate record of all controlled substances on hand on the date the inventory is taken.
  - Inventory may be taken either as of opening or as of closing on the inventory date (must be indicated on the inventory).

- **Inventory requirements**
  (21 CFR 1304.11)

  - Name of the substance
  - The finished form of the substance (i.e., 10-milligram tablet or 10-milligram concentration per fluid ounce or milliliter)
  - Number of units or volume of each finished form in each commercial container
  - Number of commercial containers of each such finished form

- **Special circumstances**

  - For any damaged, defective or impure substances waiting for disposal, substances held for quality control purposes, or substances maintained for extemporaneous compounding) the inventories shall include the following:
    - Name of the substance
    - Total quantity of the substance to the nearest metric weight unit or the total number of units of the finished form
    - The reason for the substance being maintained

Special Situations

- **Emergencies:**

  - Schedule II substances:
    - Oral orders can be given to dispense a limited quantity
    - Within 7 days of authorization, a written prescription must be delivered to the dispensing pharmacy.

  - Partial fills
    - Patients cannot request a partial fill.
    - May be done if the pharmacy lacks the full supply to fill.
    - Must be filled within 72 hours, and if it extends beyond, a new prescription is required.

- **Refills:**

  - Schedule I & II: None
  - Schedule III & IV: Based on the issue date of the prescription, may be refilled no more than 5 times in 6 months
  - Schedule V: Based on prescribers' instructions unless different by state law

- **Buprenorphine**

    - According to the Substance Abuse and Mental Health Services Administration (SAMHSA) and DEA guidance in the Consolidated Appropriations Act, 2023, prescribers are no longer required to have an X-waiver DEA number.
        - Buprenorphine is now a Schedule III.
        - Reporting requirements are no longer required.
        - No patient caps, so the prescriber can support as many patients as possible.

    - Any prescriber with a valid DEA number can initiate treatment of an opioid use disorder with buprenorphine.

    - New or renewing DEA registration for prescribing authority requires at least one of the following:
        - 8 hours of training on opioid or other substance use disorders for practitioners renewing or newly applying for registration from the DEA to prescribe any Schedule II-V controlled medications.
        - Board certification in addiction medicine or addiction psychiatry from the American Board of Medical Specialties, American Board of Addiction Medicine, or the American Osteopathic Association.
        - Graduation within five years and status in good standing from medical, advanced practice nursing, or physician assistant school in the US, including completion of an opioid or other substance use disorder curriculum of at least 8 hours.

    - The applicability of this regulation update depends on the state of the practice and its regulations related to buprenorphine.

    - No changes to methadone requirements.

FEDERAL LAW & REGULATIONS – HIPAA

HIPAA was created as a set of security standards and general requirements for protecting health information while at the same time allowing adjustments and changes in technology.

The US Department of HHS facilitates this with rules outlined in the following:
- *Standards for Privacy of PHI*
- *Security Standards for the Protection of ePHI*

Health Insurance Portability and Accountability Act (HIPAA)

- Established in 1996 by the US Department of Health & Human Services (HHS).

    - Also enforced by the Office of Civil Rights (OCR)

- The purpose is to protect individual privacy and individual security.

    - Before HIPAA, there was no generally accepted security standards or requirements for protecting health information. Around this time, technology changed from paper charts to electronic medical records, creating additional potential security risks.

The Privacy Rule

- *Standards for Privacy of Individually Identified Health Information*

- National standards that regulate the use of disclosures of health information called protected health information (PHI) to covered entities without the patient's permission.

- Also, establishes standards for patient's privacy rights to help them understand and control "how" their health information is used.

- Attempts to create a balance to assure the patient's health information is properly protected while also allowing for the flow of health information needed to provide & promote high-quality healthcare.

- **The privacy rule applies to any of the below who transmit health information in electronic form in connection with a transaction:**

    - Health plans
    - Healthcare clearinghouses
    - Healthcare providers
    - Business associates

- **Individually Identifiable Health Information:**

    - An individual's past, present, or future physical/mental health/condition.
    - The provision of healthcare to the individual
    - The past, present, or future payment for the provision of the individual's healthcare
    - Includes related demographic data that could be used to identify the person

- **De-identified Health Information:**

  - Neither identifies nor provides a reasonable basis to identify an individual
  - There are no restrictions on the use or disclosure.
  - Two ways to de-identify information include the following:
    - A formal determination by a qualified statistician.
    - Removal of specified identifiers of the individual and the individual's relatives, household members, and employers.

- **A covered entity is required to disclose PHI in only 2 situations:**

  - To individuals (or their representatives)
  - To HHS when undertaking a compliance investigation, review, or enforcement action

- **Uses and disclosures of PHI by a covered entity may occur without the persons' authorization for the following circumstances:**

  - To the individual
  - For treatment, payment, and healthcare operations
  - With an opportunity to agree or object
  - Incident to an otherwise permitted use and disclosure
  - Public interest and benefit activities
  - Limited data set for research, public health, or healthcare operations

- **The covered entity must obtain authorization if the disclosure is not for treatment.**

The Security Rule

- *Security Standards for the Protection of Electronic Protected Health Information*

- Set national regulations that protect health information that is held or electronically transmitted

- It operationalizes the protections contained in the Privacy Rule by addressing the technical and non-technical safeguards that organizations call "covered entities."

- The goal was to protect the privacy of PHI while allowing covered entities to adopt new technologies to improve the quality and efficiency of patient care.

- **Requirements of covered entities:**

  - Ensure the confidentiality, integrity, and availability of all e-PHI they create, receive, maintain or transmit
  - Identify and protect against reasonably anticipated threats to the security or integrity of the information
  - Protect against reasonably anticipated, impermissible uses or disclosures
  - Ensure compliance by their workforce

Health Information Technology For Economic And Clinical Health Act (HITECH)

- **American Recovery and Reinvestment Act (ARRA)**

  - HITECH was passed with the 2009 economic stimulus plan as part of the ARRA.
  - Initially proposed and passed to stimulate the use of electronic health records and supporting technology in healthcare
  - HIPAA was also impacted to widen the scope of privacy and security in using electronic health records.

- **Electronic Health Records (EHR)**

  - HITECH advanced the use of EHR at acute care hospitals from 10% to 96% in 2015.
  - E-prescribing, prescription drug monitoring programs (PMP), direct messaging between patients and providers, and patient-generated data are meaningful applications of EHR in exchanging health information.

⚖️ **Law Pearl**

✓ *HITECH is a new advancement in medical law. You have likely encountered benefits of this regulation by being able to access your own medical records. MyChart is EPIC's patient-based system that allows patients to view medical records, communicate with their healthcare team, and interact proactively for better health.*

21st Century Cures Act

- Mandates hospitals and doctors to make health records easily accessible by patients.

- Exemptions exist, specifically preventing access in the following circumstances:

    - Psychotherapy notes that are separated from the rest of the individual's medical record
    - Information compiled in reasonable anticipation of, or for use in, a civil, criminal, or administrative action or proceeding.
    - If the healthcare provider believes that a patient will harm another person or themselves as a result of reading the information
    - If the healthcare provider believes they must protect the security of another person's electronic health information

Informed Consent of Minors

- In each of the 50 states and the District of Columbia, a minor (under the age of full legal rights and responsibilities) has the right to provide informed consent to receive STD and/or HIV services without the consent, knowledge, or involvement of a parent or guardian.

    - This applies even if the state's law is silent on this regulation.

- State laws can define further restrictions or expansions of this federal law.

    - May explicitly allow a minor to give informed consent to receive STD diagnosis, treatment, and/or prevention.
    - May explicitly allow a minor to give informed consent to HIV testing, treatment, and/or prophylaxis, including pre-exposure prophylaxis (PrEP)
    - May allow a minor to give informed consent to general healthcare, services, or procedures.

MPJE

Review Course

Federal & General Topic Reviews

Pharmacy Practice for MPJE

FEDERAL LAW & REGULATIONS – COLOR BOOK REFERENCES

Red Book – Toxicology/safety of food ingredients
Orange Book – Therapeutic equivalency
Purple Book – Biological biosimilarity and interchangeability
Yellow Book – International travel
Pink Book – Vaccine-preventable diseases

Red Book

- **"Toxicological Principles for the Safety Assessment of Food Ingredients"**

    - **A document published by the FDA that lists its recommendations for the minimum set of toxicological data normally needed for evaluating the safety of direct food additives.**

    - **Guidance document with the purpose of assisting stakeholders in:**
        - Assessing the need for toxicity studies.
        - Designing, conducting, and reporting outcomes of toxicity studies.
        - Completing statistical analyses of data.
        - Reviewing histological data.
        - Submitting the above information to the FDA as a component of evaluating the safety of food ingredients.

    - **Uses structure-activity relationships of chemicals to assign categories to food additives.**
        - Low-potential toxic additives are considered category A.
        - Unknown or intermediate toxicity additives are category B.
        - High-order toxicity additives are category C.

    - **Concern levels are relative measures of the degree to which the use of the additive might be hazardous to human health.**
        - The levels range from Level I (lowest possible risk) to Level III (highest risk).
        - Initial or more extensive testing recommendations are listed with these Levels.

    - **FDA utilizes this data and information submitted by the sponsor related to the safety of a new additive or use of an additive generally recognized as safe (GRAS) to independently determine that the intended use is consistent with the safety standards of no harm.**

Orange Book

- **Approved drug products with therapeutic equivalence evaluations**

    - Historically, it was the "Orange Book" in printed format.
    - Now, it is replaced with the "Electronic Orange Book" (EOB), which is a living electronic document that is continuously updated.

- **Identifies drugs that have been FDA-approved and are the subject of an application with approval that has not been withdrawn for safety or efficacy reasons.**

    - No official FDA actions affect products' legal status under the FD&C Act.
    - Independent of any regulatory action taken against a drug product.

- **Contains therapeutic equivalence evaluations for approved multisource prescription drug products.**

    - Designed to serve as public information and advice to agencies, prescribers, and pharmacists to promote public education in drug product selection and reduction of health care costs.

- **Four parts, including the addendum, consist of the following:**

    - Approved prescription drug products with therapeutic equivalence evaluations
    - Approved over-the-counter (OTC) drug products not covered under OTC monographs and that cannot be marketed without NDAs or ANDAs
    - Drug products with approval under the FD&C Act administered by the Center for Biologics Evaluation and Research (CBER)
    - A cumulative list of approved products that have never been marketed are for exportation or military use, have been discontinued from marketing and not determined to have been withdrawn due to safety or efficacy reasons, or have had their approvals withdrawn for other than safety or efficacy reasons after being discontinued from marketing.
    - The addendum includes patent and exclusivity information for the Prescription, OTC, Discontinued Drug Product Lists, and Drug Products with Approval (FD&C Act Section 505).

- **The Orange Book provides core components of drug information, including:**

    - **Pharmaceutical equivalents are defined as drugs with identical dosage forms and route(s) of administration that contain identical amounts of the same active drug ingredient(s).**
        - Meet the same compendial or other standard of identity, strength, quality, and purity, and, if appropriate, content uniformity, disintegration times, and/or dissolution rates.

    - **Pharmaceutical alternatives are drug products containing identical therapeutic moieties or their precursors that do not necessarily have the same quantity or dosage form or the same salt or ester.**
        - An example would be tenofovir disoproxil fumarate and tenofovir alafenamide fumarate.

    - **Therapeutic equivalents are pharmaceutical equivalents where bioequivalence has been demonstrated.**
        - Therefore, they can be expected to have the same clinical effect and safety profile when administered to patients under the conditions specified in the labeling.

- Bioequivalent:
  - AA (conventional)
  - AB (actual or potential bioequivalence problems have been resolved with adequate in vivo and/or in vitro evidence supporting bioequivalence).
    - Can range between AB1-4
    - AN (aerosolization)
    - AO (injectable oil solutions)
    - AP (injectable aqueous solutions)
    - AT (topical)

  - Not therapeutically equivalent
    - BC (extended-release capsule/injectable/tablet)
    - BD (documented bioequivalence problems)
    - BE (delayed-release)
    - BN (aerosol-nebulized)
    - BP (potential bioequivalence problems)
    - BR (enemas or suppositories)
    - BS (common deficiencies)
    - BT (topical)
    - BX (data insufficient for therapeutic equivalence)
    - B* (undetermined)

- **Strength refers to the amount of drug substance contained in, delivered, or deliverable from a drug product.**

- **Bioavailability is the rate and extent to which the active ingredient or moiety is absorbed and becomes available at the site of drug action.**

- **Bioequivalence is the absence of a significant difference in the rate and extent to which the active ingredient or moiety in pharmaceutical equivalents or alternatives becomes available at the site of drug action when administered at the same molar dose under similar conditions in an appropriately designed study.**

Purple Book

- Lists FDA-licensed biological products with reference exclusivity and biosimilarity or interchangeability evaluations.

- Prior to 2020, existed as 2 lists from the Center for Drug Evaluation and Research (CDER) and CBER.

- Contains all information on FDA-licensed biological, biosimilar, and interchangeable biological products, as well as FDA-licensed allergenic, cellular, and gene therapies, hematologic products, and vaccine products regulated by the CDER.

- Definitions:

  - A reference product is a single biological product (under FDA section 351(a) of the Public Health Service [PHS] Act) against which a proposed biological product is evaluated in an application.
  - Biosimilar describes biological products having similar reference products, notwithstanding minor differences in clinically inactive components, and no clinically meaningful difference in the product's safety, purity, and potency.
  - Interchangeable biological products are biosimilar to the reference product and are expected to produce the same clinical result in any patient.

- Product exclusivity, under the PHS section 351(k)(7), describes periods of reference product exclusivity from the date the reference product is first licensed.

  - The reference product must be eligible for the periods of reference product exclusivity.
  - Must not occur until 4 years after the reference product was first licensed.
  - It cannot be effective until 12 years after the reference product was first licensed, also known as the exclusivity expiration date.
    - Two additional years of pediatric exclusivity can be granted.

- Contains information for multiple users (i.e., patients, the general public, healthcare providers, manufacturers, and researchers).

Yellow Book

- CDC Health Information For International Travel is published every two years.

- Resource for health professionals providing care to international travelers.

- Contains the US government's travel health guidelines

    - Pretravel vaccine recommendations
    - Destination-specific health advice
    - Easy-to-reference maps, tables, and charts
    - Additional content includes guidance on providing travel health care remotely via telemedicine, discussion of legal issues facing clinicians providing travel health care, rapid diagnostic tests for infectious diseases (ID), new FDA-approved antimalarial drugs, road traffic safety advice for travelers, and recommendations for treating ID related to antimicrobial resistance.

Pink Book

- Epidemiology and Prevention of Vaccine-Preventable Diseases

- Produced by the Communication and Education Branch, National Center for Immunization and Respiratory Diseases, and Centers for Disease Control and Prevention.

- Informs physicians, nurses, nurse practitioners, physician assistants, pharmacists, and other healthcare professionals regarding the most comprehensive information on routinely used vaccines and the diseases they prevent.

- The main content provides general immunization recommendations, vaccine safety, storage and handling, and administration information.

    - Detailed information is also given about vaccine-preventable diseases, including disease pathogenesis, clinical features, epidemiology, and secular trends in the US.
    - Vaccine information, including vaccine characteristics, schedule and use, efficacy, safety, and contraindications and precautions, is also included.
    - Four appendices provide reference materials.

FEDERAL LAW & REGULATIONS – FDA Recall

FDA Recall

- Recalls are actions taken to remove a product overseen by the FDA from the market.

  - Recalls can be done under a firm's initiative, by request from the FDA, or by the FDA order under statutory authority.

- The FDA collects recall information and completes health hazard evaluations to determine the risk associated with a product and the need for a recall.

- The recall process is a partnership between the manufacturer and the FDA.

  - Develop a recall strategy based on the health hazard risk and other factors such as distribution patterns and market availability.
  - Determine the need for public warnings.
  - Enter a partnership with a recalling firm for public notification.

- Recall classifications are established based on the level of risk.

  - **Class I Recall**
    - Reasonable probability of serious adverse health consequences or death from the exposure or use of a violative product
      - Examples include microbial contamination of a sterile product, lack of sterility assurance, and presence of particulate matter.

  - **Class II Recall**
    - Exposure to a violative product has a risk, albeit low, of temporary or medically reversible adverse health consequences or a slight risk of serious adverse health effects
      - An example is stability data not supporting expiration.

  - **Class III Recall**
    - Rare or very low risk of adverse health consequences from exposure to a violative product.
      - Examples include speculation of a potential risk or defective containers.

  - **Market Withdrawal**
    - Product removal from the market due to a minor violation is not subject to FDA legal action.

  - **Medical Device Safety Alert**
    - Due to the unreasonable risk of substantial harm from a medical device

FEDERAL LAW & REGULATIONS – HEALTH SYSTEM ACCREDITATION & CERTIFICATION

Healthcare systems have several accreditations and/or certifications that they must obtain and maintain to not only operate but to ensure a certain level of quality and safety while also receiving payment for services rendered.

Accreditations, certifications, and regulatory agencies enforce various laws to help regulate healthcare activities.

Health-System Practice

- Governed and regulated by several organizations and accrediting bodies

- Professional organizations also help set standards of practice (i.e., within pharmacy, nursing, etc.).

- Benefits:

    - Improve participation in programs paying for healthcare, such as:
        - Insurance companies
        - Government agencies
    - Attract good healthcare staff.
    - May be exempt from other inspections.

- Government & non-government agencies look for these accreditations and compliance to allow institutions to participate in government programs.

    - These are called "Conditions of Participation (CoPs)."
    - Government agencies include Medicare and Medicaid.
    - Non-government agencies include Kaiser.

Accrediting Bodies

- The Joint Commission (JCAHO)

    - The primary accrediting organization for setting standards for the operation of hospitals and other healthcare organizations and programs, including:
        - Ambulatory Care
        - Assisted Living
        - Behavioral Health
        - Critical Access Hospitals
        - Home Care
        - Hospitals
        - Laboratory Services
        - Nursing Care Centers
        - Office-Based Surgery

    - State governments recognize JCAHO accreditation for licensure and Medicare/Medicaid reimbursements.
    - Three-year accreditation cycle (laboratories every 2 years)
    - Accreditation determined from onsite surveys

- Accreditation decisions, accreditation dates, and any standards cited for improvement are public knowledge.
- Accreditation "grade" is unknown, but most organizations deemed to comply with all or most of the applicable standards are awarded the decision of accreditation.

- Surveys occur 18 to 39 months after the organization's previous unannounced survey.
    - Survey findings are reported to the institution for improvement.
    - Provides information to aid healthcare professionals decision-making based on best standards but not meant to be a "cookbook" approach.

- **Also developed National Patient Safety Goals (NPSG)**
    - NPSG.03 is specific to drug therapy and includes the following:
        - NPSG.03.04.01 – Before a procedure, label medicines that are not labeled.
        - NPSG.03.05.01 – Take extra care with patients who take medicines to thin their blood.
        - NPSG.03.06.01 – Record and pass along correct information about a patient's medicines. Find out what medicines the patient is taking. Compare those medicines to new medicines given to the patient. Give the patient written information about the medicines they need to take. Tell the patient it is important to bring their up-to-date medicine list every time they visit a doctor.

- **Other JCAHO-established standards include components of:**
    - Medication management
    - Infection control
    - Patient care
    - Medical records
    - Safety and security
    - Education
    - Performance improvement
    - Environment of care

- **JCAHO visit and preparation resources include:**
    - The Joint Commission's Accreditation Survey Activity Guide for Healthcare Organizations.
    - Comprehensive Accreditation Manual for Hospitals: The Official Handbook (CAMH).

- **Center for Improvement in Healthcare (CIHQ)**

    - An accrediting organization for the operation of hospitals

- **Healthcare Facilities Accreditation Program (HFAP)**

    - Accreditation for the operation of hospitals set by the accrediting organization from the American Osteopathy Association (AOA).

Patient Safety Bodies

- **Agency For Healthcare Research And Quality (AHRQ)**

    - Agency within the U.S. Department of Health and Human Services
    - Produces evidence to make healthcare safer, higher quality, and more accessible, equitable, and affordable.
    - Works within the U.S. Department of Health and Human Services and with other partners to ensure the evidence is understood and used.
    - AHRQ Quality Indicators track clinical performance and outcomes with standardized, evidence-based healthcare quality measures.

- **Report Cards**

    - Monitor quality of care and are accessible public information.
    - Provide tools to empower healthcare consumers to select higher-quality caregivers and institutions.

- **Star Ratings**

    - Summarizes hospital quality information, i.e., readmissions and deaths after heart attacks or pneumonia.
    - Summarizes a variety of measures across 5 areas of quality into a single-star rating for each hospital.
    - The top 5 measured groups include:
        - Mortality
        - Safety of care
        - Readmission
        - Patient experience
        - Timely and effective care

FEDERAL LAW & REGULATIONS – NARROW THERAPEUTIC INDEX DRUG REGULATION

Narrow *therapeutic index (NTI) drugs have a narrow margin for their safe and effective use in clinical practice. They also have smaller therapeutic indexes (TI).*

NTI drugs must be dosed more carefully with closer patient monitoring.

Federal Criteria for NTI Drugs

- **Narrow Therapeutic Index (NTI) Drugs:**

  - The safe and effective use of these drugs requires specific dosing and close monitoring of the patient.
  - FDA sets the criteria and determines this list of drugs.
  - Described as drugs with narrow therapeutic ratios.
    - The difference between the median lethal dose (LD50) and the median effective dose (ED50) is < 2-fold.
    - The difference between the minimum toxic concentration (MTC) and the minimum effective concentration (MEC) in the blood is < 2-fold.
    - The FDA allows most drugs to have a variability limit of 90 to 110% of the claim on the label.

Calculating the Therapeutic Index

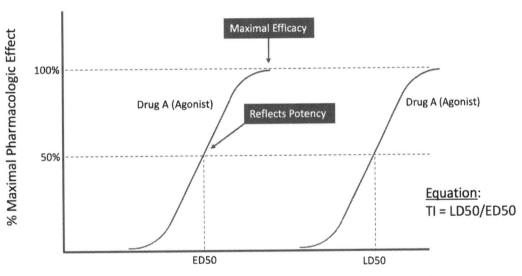

Logarithmic Concentration of Drug A (Agonist)

- **The higher the TI, the "safer" the drug**

- **Inversely, the smaller the TI, the greater the risk of toxicity**

FDA's List of NTI Drugs

FDA List of NTI Drugs	
Carbamazepine	Phenytoin
Cyclosporine	Procainamide
Digoxin	Phenytoin
Ethosuximide	Tacrolimus
Levothyroxine	Theophylline
Lithium	Warfarin

Drugs Needing Therapeutic Drug Monitoring

Drugs Requiring Therapeutic Drug Monitoring				
Drug	SE / ADRs	Narrow TI	Efficacy	Compliance
Aminoglycosides	✓		✓	
Carbamazepine	✓	✓	✓	✓
Cyclosporine	✓		±	✓
Digoxin	✓	✓		✓
Dilantin (phenytoin)	✓		✓	✓
Flucytosine	✓		±	
Itraconazole			✓	✓
Lithium	✓	✓	±	✓
Phenobarbital	✓		✓	✓
Protease Inhibitors			✓	✓
Procainamide	✓	✓		✓
Valproic Acid	✓		✓	✓
Vancomycin	✓		✓	
Warfarin	✓	✓		

FEDERAL LAW & REGULATIONS – OTC & NONPRESCRIPTION MEDICATIONS

OTC or nonprescription medications are considered safe or suitable for use without the supervision of a physician and require some Federal government oversight.

Complete a medication use evaluation at each visit that includes OTC medications. As appropriate, educate and counsel the patient.

General Information

- Over-the-counter (OTC) or nonprescription medications are considered safe or suitable for use without the supervision of a physician.

- Used for self-diagnosed conditions.

- Contain labeling with adequate directions for self-use.

Labeling

- **Information and Contents:**

    - Contains a *Drug Facts* section.
    - The goal is to aid the consumer in choosing the proper product for the condition and to have enough information to self-manage.
    - Must contain certain information in the same format for consistency.
    - Failing to include all components is "misbranding."

Section	Description
Active Ingredients	- Amount per unit dose
Uses	- Based on disease or symptoms to prevent or treat
Warnings	- When to not use or consult with a physician - Possible side effects and drug interactions - When to stop and consult with a physician
Inactive Ingredients	- List all substances (including coloring or flavors)
Purpose	- Provides a general action of the drug (i.e., decongestant)
Directions for Use	- How to take - How often to take per day - Duration of treatment
Other Info	- Proper storage - If the product contains calcium, potassium, magnesium, or sodium - Lot number and expiration date - Net quantities of a packaged product - What to do in an overdose

- **General Messages:**

  - Special Populations (Pregnant & Nursing Mothers)

    - If the OTC product will be for systemic use and if the product is not already intended to benefit the fetus or nursing infant, then the label must state the following:
      - "As with any drug, if you are pregnant or nursing a baby, seek the advice of a health professional before using this product."
    - If the OTC product is to be taken by mouth or rectally, then it must also contain the following:
      - "It is especially important not to use this product during the last three months of pregnancy unless specifically directed to do so by a doctor."

Packaging Considerations

- **Tamper-Resistant Packaging Act**

  - Now called tamper-evident packaging
  - Several cases of deliberate poisoning
  - The goal is to prevent intentional contamination of OTC products.
  - Exceptions to the rule:
    - Aerosol products
    - Products not available to the public (i.e., clinics only)
    - Lozenges
    - First aid kits

> ⚖️ **Law Pearl**
>
> ✓ Tamper-resistant packaging was created in response to the tragic 1982 series of poisonings.
> ✓ From tampering with capsules of Extra-Strength Tylenol, a yet to be identified individual replaced them with lethal potassium cyanide tablets.
> ✓ A total of 7 people in the Chicago area died, with additional deaths occurring from copycat attacks around the country.

Practice Considerations

- **Potential issues related to drug interactions**

  - **Antacids**
    - pH changes and bioavailability
      - Atazanavir
      - Dasatinib
      - Erlotinib
      - Levothyroxine

  - **CYP450 Interactions**
    - Cimetidine → weak inhibitor of CYP1A2, 2C19, 3A4
    - Lansoprazole and omeprazole → inhibit clopidogrel activation

- **Potential issues related to topical application**

  - **Topical steroids**
    - Avoid around the eyes
    - Avoid placement to the face or genitals
    - Avoid use between the fingers and toes → maceration of tissue

- **Special populations**

  - **Pediatric patients**
    - If < 6 months → no NSAIDs
    - If < 2 years old → no Benadryl
    - Avoid aspirin → risk of Reye's syndrome
    - Dosing requirements

  - **Pregnant patients & nursing mothers**
    - Watch out for → NSAIDs

  - **Patients with kidney disease**

  - **Patients on anticoagulants or antiplatelets**

  - **Patient with hypertension**

  - **Patient with risks for small bowel obstruction**
    - Watch out for → laxatives

.

FEDERAL LAW & REGULATIONS – PARENTERAL DRUG THERAPY

Parenteral drug therapy is a method of medication administration that avoids the alimentary canal.

Several factors go into which route of administration is utilized.

Basic Terminology

- **Parenteral Therapy:**

    - Medications in dosage forms that are meant to be injected through the skin and into a tissue compartment or vascular space instead of being administered by mouth or the alimentary canal.

- **Rationale for Parenteral Therapy:**

    - Patient is unable to swallow.
    - Alimentary (enteral) canal cannot be used or is not functioning correctly.
    - To by-pass first-pass metabolism
    - Lack of oral bioavailability
    - Onset of drug action is time-sensitive
    - Compliance or adherence

Dosage Formulations

- **Parenteral Dosage Formulation Terminology:**

    - **Ampul**
        - A glass container with a single-use of medication
        - The glass container is gently broken at one end and may require a needle filter to extract the contents to avoid pulling glass particles into the injection device.

    - **Vial**
        - A plastic (usually) or glass container with a rubber grommet sealed closure at the top surrounded by a metal ring
        - Can be a single-use or multi-dose vial.

    - **Vehicle**
        - The liquid that contains the medication that is dissolved, suspended, or emulsified
        - The most common liquid is sterile water for injection (USP), but may sometimes include ethanol or oils.

    - **Total Parenteral Nutrition (TPN)**
        - Also referred to as hyperalimentation
        - Used for patients unable to consume nutrients and calories enterally.

Administration Considerations

- **Considerations for preparation and dispensing:**

  - Try to dispense or have admixtures that are ready-to-use.
  - Have a standardized process for compounding medications sterilely and free of distractions.
  - Label IV admixtures in a standard format.
  - Ensure the competency of those preparing the medication.

- **Special considerations before administration of parenteral therapy:**

  - Have double checks in place.
  - Have standardized IV medication administration recommendations to minimize errors from distractions or interruptions.
  - Ensure personnel competency to administer the IV medications.
  - Limit the number of steps to prepare IV medications.
  - Establish plans for antidotes and ongoing monitoring procedures.
  - Standard Precautions
    - Follow guidelines meant to protect the healthcare worker who has occupational exposure to bloodborne pathogens or bodily fluids.
    - All bodily fluids should generally be considered infectious.

Routes of Administration

- **Epidural:**

  - This space is superior to the dura mater and spinal cord but inferior to the ligamentum flavum where the CSF is located.
  - Should be administered by strict aseptic technique given access to the CNS.

- **Intra-arterial (IA):**

  - Generally, this route is NOT advised and can lead to serious complications to the end organ of that artery.
  - Examples:
    - Directly administered tPA for clots for conditions such as STEMI, acute ischemic stroke, submassive or massive PE with hemodynamic instability, or acute peripheral arterial occlusion

- **Intra-articular:**

  - Administration of the medication directly into the joint space
  - A strict aseptic technique should be followed to avoid the risk of introducing bacteria into the joint, which can lead to a septic joint.
  - In some cases, fluid extraction may be required to avoid inserting too much fluid into the space.
    - May also have a volume limitation based on the size of the joint space available.

- **Intradermal:**

  - Administration of the medication directly into the superficial layer of the skin between the dermis and epidermis
  - Absorption is slower than SubQ or IM.

- Limit volume of administration to ~ 0.1 mL
- Examples:
  - Tuberculin skin test for TB evaluation
  - Vaccines or IgG (i.e., rabies)

- **Intraosseous (IO):**

  - Administration of the medication directly into the bone marrow
  - Easy to insert and set up
  - Absorption is rapid and similar to IV.
  - No significant limitation to the volume of administration
  - Consider premedication with IO lidocaine because of the potential for pain.
  - Examples:
    - ACLS / Codes
    - Unable to obtain IV access and emergency treatment needed
  - Note:
    - Avoid the use of a bone that is injured.
    - Apply infusions under a pressure bag.

- **Intrathecal:**

  - Administration of the medication directly into the spinal canal or subarachnoid space
  - Difficult to do and more invasive
  - Requires strict aseptic technique
  - Examples:
    - Anesthesia
    - Chemotherapy

- **Intramuscular (IM):**

  - Administration of the medication directly into the muscle
  - One-time medication administration
  - Locations of administration:
    - Upper arm (in adults)
    - Thigh (especially in pediatric patients)
    - Gluteal muscles (in adults)
  - Volume limitation of 2-3 mL to the upper arm and no more than 5 mL in the gluteal muscle of an adult
  - The absorption rate is less than IV but faster than SubQ and intradermal.

- **Intravenous (IV):**

  - Medication administration directly into the vascular space is the most common route in the hospital.
  - Provides 100% bioavailability and rapid onset of action (when needed).
  - The fluid volume can be small or large depending on the vessel cannulated with an IV.
  - Duration of IV placement:
    - Short, peripheral: replace every 72-96 hrs
    - Midline, peripheral: replace every 7 – 30 days
    - Central lines: last weeks up to 1 year
  - Central line vs. Peripheral IVs:
    - Central lines can receive chemotherapy, irritants, TPN, medications with pH < 5 or > 9 or osmolarity > 600 mOsm

Fast Facts

✓ Administering vinka alkaloids intrathecally is a fatal medication error.
✓ Intraosseous medications are routine and can be done in awake patients with a lidocaine 2% 5 mL flush instead of saline.
✓ Rabies immune globulin must be administered intradermally around the wound, or in a site distant from the rabies vaccine administration.

- Peripheral IV lines can receive medications with moderate pH of 5 to 9 and parenteral nutrition up to 900 mOsm/L.
  - Generally, avoid vesicants or irritating drugs (dopamine, chemo).
- Risks:
  - Pain and venous irritation
  - Infiltration or extravasation of infusion into the tissue
  - Line infection
  - Most medication suspensions cannot be given this route.

- **Subcutaneous (SubQ):**

  - Administration of the medication directly into the tissue beneath the skin and above the muscle
  - Locations of administration:
    - Upper arm
    - Thigh
    - Abdomen
  - The absorption rate is less than IM or IV but faster than intradermal
  - Less commonly utilized for continuous infusions

- **Special considerations for the administration of parenteral therapy:**

  - Duration of stability once mixed or prepared
  - Protection from light
  - Need for an IV pump
  - The concentration of the parenteral mixture
  - Suspension or solution
  - Ability or need to titrate
  - Need for a filter (0.22, 0.45, or 5-micron filters) to capture particulate matter
  - Binding of the drug to plastic tubing
  - Latex allergies
  - Size of the blood vessel in relation to the medication being administered (i.e., IV access)
    - Ability to cause phlebitis
    - Risk of infiltration (i.e., under pressure) or extravasation

Disposal

- Disposal of parenteral drug therapy:

  - All needles or syringes that may contain blood or bodily fluids should NOT be recapped
  - Place in a "sharps" container which is a nonpermeable, puncture-resistant, tamper-proof biohazard container

FEDERAL LAW & REGULATIONS – THERAPEUTIC EQUIVALENCE & GENERIC SUBSTITUTION

The Orange Book is now the Electronic Orange Book pharmacists use to determine if one drug product is therapeutically equivalent for generic substitution.

Given the growing number of biologic agents on the market, there are also rules for substitutions in what are now called biosimilars.

Basic Terminology and Descriptions

- **Pharmaceutical Equivalents**

    - Drug products that are considered to be identical dosage forms, route(s) of administration, and which contain an identical active drug ingredient.
    - Products can vary or differ in the inactive ingredients, dosage form shape, scoring, mechanism of release, packaging, excipients, expiration date, and labeling.

- **Pharmaceutical Alternatives**

    - A drug product that contains an identical therapeutic moiety or its precursor but may not be the same dosage amount, dosage form, salt, or ester.
        - Example: A single manufacturer with a product line with different dosage forms and strengths.

- **Bioequivalence**

    - When drug products are administered under the same molar dose and similar conditions in a controlled study environment, there is no presence of significant differences in the rate and extent at which the drug is available at the site of action.

- **Biosimilars**

    - Unique biologic drugs are derived from living organisms by recombinant technology and are highly similar to the reference product.

- **Therapeutic Equivalents**

    - Products approved by the FDA that are pharmaceutical equivalents where bioequivalence has been documented that are expected to have the same clinical effect and safety profile when used in the same medical conditions.
    - Therapeutically equivalent drug products meet the following general criteria:
        - Approved as safe and effective
        - Are pharmaceutical equivalents
        - Are bioequivalent
        - Adequately labeled
        - Manufactured in compliance with GMP regulations

The Orange Book

- **Determining therapeutic equivalence**

    - Historically, it was the "Orange Book," printed in book format.
        - The purpose was to find and evaluate therapeutic equivalence for various pharmaceutical products and assign codes to denote the equivalence.
    - Now replaced with the "Electronic Orange Book" (EOB).
        - A living electronic document that is continuously updated

- **Basic Criteria for Approval of a Generic Product**

    - All generic substitutes must also be compared to a reference product and demonstrate the following:
        - Same mechanism of action
        - Same route of administration
        - Same dosage form
        - Same dosage strength
        - No difference in purity, potency, and/or safety to the reference drug

- **Methylphenidate Substitution**

    - Extended-release methylphenidate products are considered BX (Orange Book equivalency) due to the bioavailability equivalency issues between Mallinckrodt and Kudco and the Concerta product.

- See "COLOR BOOK REFERENCES" for detailed information.

Generic Substitution of Biosimilars

- **Basic definition**

    - Unique biologic drugs that are derived from living organisms by recombinant technology and are highly similar to the reference product.

- **Federal Law**

    - Biologics Price Competition and Innovation Act (BPCIA) of 2009
        - Includes a process of approving generic, small-molecule drugs under the Hatch-Waxman Act.
        - Application of generic products:
            - Apply to utilize a Biologic License Application (BLA) to fully evaluate purity, potency, and safety.
            - Apply to utilize a Biosimilar Application, which is an abbreviated evaluation.

- **Examples of Biosimilars for generic substitution can include**

    - Blood or blood component
    - Gene therapy
    - Proteins
    - Tissue
    - Vaccines

- **Published in the FDA's "Purple Book."**

FEDERAL LAW & REGULATIONS – PRESCRIPTION MEDICATIONS – FILLING & DISPENSING

While the prescription is a provider's order for a medication, the pharmacist plays an important role between the provider and the patient.

This level of checks and balances helps protect the patient from any bad outcomes or inappropriate treatment use.

General Prescription Information

- **An order to provide a patient with a specific medication.**

- **General considerations**

    - Usually is not for immediate/acute use (i.e., within the hospital, which is usually considered a medication order by a provider and can be verbal or in written/electronic form)
    - Presented on specific prescription paper or electronically submitted as a fax.
    - Written and provided by someone authorized to prescribe.

- **What is a valid prescription?**

    - Per the US Code – Title 21 829(e)(2)(A), the term "valid prescription" means a prescription that is issued for a legitimate medical purpose in the usual course of professional practice by—(i)a practitioner who has conducted at least 1 in-person medical evaluation of the patient; or (ii)a covering practitioner.

- **Who is authorized to prescribe?**

    - This is state dependent.
    - Some non-physician providers will have prescriptive limitations such as:
        - Nurse practitioners
        - Physician assistants
        - Pharmacists
    - Some providers can self-prescribe, but this excludes controlled substances.

- **Can a pharmacist refuse to fill a prescription?**

    - Yes, but it generally needs to fall within one of the following categories or situations:
        - The person prescribing the medication is not authorized to prescribe
        - Suspect that the prescription is forged or has been altered by someone other than the authorized prescriber
        - If the prescription is written for something that is considered illegal
        - The pharmacist does not have the medication to fill it
        - The pharmacist believes that the medication would be harmful to the patient
        - States with conscience clauses.

- **Prescription refills and rules**

    - Controlled substances have different rules, i.e., CII drugs cannot be refilled.
    - The pharmacist's ability to refill a prescription is based on the number of refills authorized by the prescriber.
    - Pharmacists must have a reliable way to track the refills.

- Emergency refills of a limited quantity are allowed in most cases, especially if failing to provide the medication could harm the patient.

- **Prescription management**

    - Once the prescription has been filled, it is owned by that pharmacy.
    - Prescriptions must be kept and stored.
        - The duration can vary by state.
        - The FDA states they can ask for data going back 5 years.
        - The 2003 Medicare Modernization Act states prescriptions need to be stored for 10 years.

Prescription Labels and Packaging

- **Standards for the prescription label**

    - Determined by USP 36-NF31
    - **Priority elements of the label**
        - Patient's name
        - Prescription number
        - Full generic and brand name
        - Strength
        - Clear instructions in simple language

    - **Other elements of the label**

        - Date filed
        - Expiration date
        - Quantity
        - Prescriber's name
        - Pharmacy name, address, and phone number
        - Remaining refills

    - **Font style and size**

        - Times New Roman 12 point
        - Arial 11 point

    - **Spell out the names of medications.**

        - Do not use abbreviations.

    - **Other considerations**

        - Indication or purpose (unless the patient does not want it)
        - Use the patient's preferred language when possible, but the drug name must be in English for emergency personnel to be able to read.

- **Packaging Considerations**

  - Prescription medications come in small or large bulk quantities for dispensing.

- **Labeling Considerations**

  - To help reduce medication and identification errors, the FDA and the Institute for Safe Medication Practices (ISMP) developed and published a list of look-alike medications and recommend utilizing Tall Man Lettering.
  - Tall Man Lettering examples
    - acetaZOLAMIDE vs. acetoHEXAMIDE
    - buPROPion vs. busPIRone
    - cycloSERINE vs. cycloSPORINE
    - hydrALAZINE vs. hydrOXYzine
    - vinBLAStine vs. vinCRIStine

- **Packaging to protect children from accidental poisoning**

  - Child-resistant containers for prescription products
    - Providers can provide a waiver for each prescription.
    - Patients can provide a waiver to cover more than one prescription.
    - For prescription refills, both parts of the plastic container must be replaced.
      - Glass bottles may be reused, but plastic caps must be replaced.

  - Poison Prevention Packaging Act (PPPA)
    - Under the supervision of the Consumer Product Safety Commission (CPSC)
    - Goal is to protect children < 5 years of age from accidental ingestion.
    - Example drugs under the rule:
      - All prescription drugs, especially controlled substances
      - Acetaminophen
      - Aspirin
      - Diphenhydramine
      - Fluoride
      - Ibuprofen and naproxen
      - Iron
      - Loperamide
      - Methyl salicylate
      - Minoxidil

      - Important exemptions include:
        - Acetaminophen effervescent
        - Aerosol inhalation products
        - Aspirin effervescent
        - Cholestyramine or colestipol powder
        - Isosorbide dinitrate SL or chewable tablets $\leq$ 10 mg
        - Nitroglycerin sublingual (SL) tablets
        - Oral contraceptives in dial-packages
        - Potassium supplements (unit dose only)

Patient Counseling

- **Drug utilization review (DUR)**

  - States:
    - Have them in place per CMS rules for participating in the Medicaid program.
    - Must have prospective and retrospective DUR programs in place.

  - Pharmacists:
    - A prospective DUR of the patient's written medical record is required before the prescription is dispensed to the patient. This should include:
      - Name, address, age or DOB, gender, presence of disease states, allergies, list of prior medications filled, and any comments
      - Over or under-utilization of a medication
      - Therapy duplications
      - Doses and instructions
    - Should offer to talk to the patient about anything relevant.

- **OBRA 90**

  - Mandates the requirement of offering to counsel the patient
  - Since this is part of the Medicaid program, which is run by the states, states/providers/healthcare systems have to show support for this being done to participate.
  - Federal law does not dictate what must be said, so use professional judgment.

A Note About
Calculations

The NABP does not explicitly state whether or not calculations will be on the MPJE exam in the most current competency statements. Historically, a basic knowledge of core calculations' concepts was necessary in order for a pharmacist to properly apply certain aspects of the law; this typically centered around compounding and/or properly dispensing a legal prescription order.

As such, we have chosen to include some of these core concepts related to calculations for those who feel they need this additional information where applicable to that state since this specific topic can vary from one state to another.

If you have not done so yet, PLEASE watch this short
video on how to study for the MPJE using our program.
It WILL help you.

SCAN ME

COMPOUNDING – USP 795 – NON-STERILE

USP 795 describes the minimum standards when preparing NSC for humans and animals.
Core concepts include describing the appropriate garbing, cleaning, inspecting, and labeling procedures.

Non-Sterile Compounding (NSC) Categories

- **Simple**

    - Reconstitution of commercial products requiring one or more ingredients according to the manufacturer.
    - Compounding monograph in the United States Pharmacopeia (USP)
    - Compounding method published in a peer-reviewed journal article
        - The article provides the specific quantities of all components, compounding procedure and equipment, and stability data for that formulation with appropriate beyond-use dates (BUD).
    - Examples: lisinopril oral solution, ibuprofen topical gel, and potassium bromide oral solution

- **Moderate**

    - A compound requiring special calculations or procedures to identify quantities of components in the given preparation or specific individualized dosage units.
    - No available stability data for the specific formula of a preparation
    - Examples: hydromorphone suppository, diphenhydramine troches

- **Complex**

    - A compound requiring special training, environment, facilities, equipment, and procedures to ensure appropriate therapeutic outcomes.
    - Example: ketamine transdermal and some inserts and suppositories for systemic effects

Compounding Personnel & Responsibilities

- **Personnel**

    - Compounding personnel are often pharmacists and pharmacy technicians (PT), but physicians, veterinarians, dentists, naturopaths, chiropractors, and nurses are also permitted to compound.
    - Before performing NSC, personnel must undergo training consisting of core competencies, including hand hygiene, garbing, cleaning, sanitizing, component selection, handling and transport, performing calculations, measuring and mixing, use of equipment, and documenting the compounding process.
    - Individuals involved in preparing and handling NSCs must demonstrate competency, undergo annual training, observe compounding activities routinely, and take immediate corrective actions if deficiencies are observed.
    - Maintain state-specific continuing education (CE) in drug or dietary supplement compounding, USP 797 requirements, pharmaceutical dosage forms, calculations, written prescription drug information guidelines, and quality assurance in compounding, prescription balances, and volumetric apparatuses.

- **Facility and Equipment**

    - The compounding facility must have leadership to manage personnel involved in preparing, storing, packing, and transporting all compounds and to proactively identify potential operational problems.

    - Space designated for NSC must be separate from areas not directly related to compounding and separate from areas for sterile compounding.
        - An exception to this is for hazardous NSC, which must be compounded in USP 800 areas that are not used for compounding non-hazardous NSC.
        - Depending on the site, NSC areas must be cleaned and sanitized immediately after spills or contamination or at a specific frequency.
            - Floors must be cleaned and sanitized daily.
            - Ceilings, walls, and storage shelving must be cleaned and sanitized every 3 months.

    - Equipment surfaces in contact with drug components must not be additive, reactive, or absorptive and cannot alter the quality of NSC.
        - Automated, electronic, mechanical, and other equipment used in NSC must be inspected before use and verified for accuracy at least annually or more frequently if recommended by the manufacturer.

    - Any process where the active pharmaceutical ingredient or added powder substance could become airborne must occur inside a containment device (i.e., containment ventilated enclosure [CVE] or powder containment hood).
        - CVE areas must be equipped with an exhaust alarm that is certified every 6 months.
        - CVE work surfaces must be cleaned at the beginning and end of each shift, between compounding different drugs, after spills, and when surface contamination is known or suspected.
        - Equipment used in compounding operations must be cleaned before and after each use.

Non-Sterile Compounding Principles

- Bulk containers should be appropriately labeled with Occupational Safety and Health Administration (OSHA) hazard communication labels.

- Safety Data Sheets (SDS) should be available to compounding personnel for all relevant drugs and chemicals.

- All equipment used in compounding must be clean, properly maintained, and used appropriately.

- NSC environment is maintained in a suitable condition with implemented procedures to prevent cross-contamination.
    - High-risk medications requiring cross-contamination prevention include hazardous drugs and known allergens (i.e., sulfa compounds or beta-lactams).

- Compounding area is restricted to the authorized compounding personnel.

- Compounding preparation, procedures, and storage are appropriately documented.

- Hand Hygiene

    - Hand hygiene with clean clothing is required for compounding.
        - Personal outer garments, including bandanas, coats, hats, jackets, scarves, sweaters, or vests, must be removed.
        - All exposed jewelry, piercings, and other exposed elements on the hand or wrist that can interfere with the effectiveness of the garb or hand hygiene must be removed.
    - Hand hygiene must be performed when entering the compounding area and re-entering after any exit.
    - Hand hygiene procedure:
        - Hands and forearms up to the elbows must be washed with soap and water for at least 30 seconds and then dried completely with disposable towels or wipes.
        - After hands and forearms are thoroughly dried, gloves may be donned.
    - Hand hygiene must be performed before starting any new NSC during compounding.
        - If hand hygiene and gloves are already being worn, hands should be washed with gloves on.
        - Gloves must be changed if they have been compromised.

- Garbing

    - Gloves are required for all NSC activities, with masks, gowns, hair covers, or shoe covers deemed appropriate depending on the compound being performed to protect the compounding personnel from chemical exposures and contamination.
    - For non-soiled gowns, when exiting the compounding area, they can be removed and retained in the compounding area for re-donning during the same work shift.
        - Does not apply to gloves, shoe covers, hair covers, face masks, or head coverings.
    - Non-disposable garb (i.e., goggles, respirators) must be cleaned with isopropyl alcohol 70% before re-use.

Components

- **Component Selection**

    - Active pharmaceutical ingredients (API) must be manufactured by an FDA-registered facility and accompanied by a valid certificate of analysis (COA).
    - Purified water, or its equivalent, must be used to reconstitute conventionally manufactured NSC when water quality is not stated in the manufacturer's labeling.
    - Before use, the compounding staff must visually re-inspect all components besides the initial inspection upon delivery.
        - If there is any identity, strength, purity, or quality issue, the component must be rejected and immediately discarded or labeled as rejected and segregated to prevent use before disposal.

- **Component Spill and Disposal**

    - The SDS's chemical hazard and disposal information must be reviewed and updated annually.
    - Spill kits must be stored in the compounding area.
    - Spills should be immediately managed by following the facility's standard operating procedure for NSC component spills and disposals.

- **Beyond Use Date (BUD)**

    - Expiration date refers to when a conventionally manufactured drug product is expected to maintain its labeled identity, strength, purity, and quality.
        - Not appropriate for NSC because the types of full stability studies conducted by manufacturers to establish expiration dates are not normally performed.
    - BUD is the time period after which an NSC cannot be used and can be calculated in number of hours, days, or months.
        - Day 1 is the date it was compounded.
        - BUD cannot be beyond the expiration date.
        - Determined based on the physical stability properties of the API and any other added substance, compatibility of the container-closure system of the finished product, degradation of the container closure system, and potential for microbial growth in the NSC.
    - BUD listed in the USP-NF monograph for the preparation can be used unless a shorter BUD is required based on the following dosage forms:
        - Capsules, tablets, granules, powders – 180 days (room temperature)
        - Preserved aqueous – 30 days (room temperature)
        - Non-aqueous – 90 days (room temperature)
        - Non-preserved aqueous – 14 days (refrigerator)

- **Storage and Transport**

    - Storage room temperature must be monitored manually at least once daily or on days compounding is performed using continuous temperature monitoring.
    - Recorded temperatures must be documented in a stored log and be retrievable.
    - Humidity of the storage room temperature must be ≤ 60 %.

Standard Operating Principles (SOP)

- NSC facilities must have an SOP for all elements of compounding operations.

  - Immediately recognize potential deviations, errors, or problems related to the compounding process, equipment, facilities, materials, personnel, or testing materials that can result in contamination or other adverse impacts on NSC quality.

- **Master Formulation Record (MFR)**

  - Name, strength, and dosage of the NSC
  - Physical description of the final NSC
  - Ingredient identities and amounts, container closure system, and characteristics of the components
  - Instructions for preparing NSC, including necessary equipment
  - BUD assignment and storage requirements
  - Reference source of the BUD and storage requirements
  - Quality control procedures and any other information needed to describe operations

- **Compounding Records**

  - Document required to be made for compounding of each NSC.
  - Name, strength, and dosage form of the NSC, physical description of the final NSC, MFR reference used, any deviations from the MFR, date and time of preparation, assigned internal identification number, signature or initials of individuals involved in each step, name, vendor or manufacturer, lot number, and expiration date of each ingredient and container–closure system.
  - Weight or measurement of each ingredient, documentation of calculations made to determine and verify quantities or concentrations of components, documentation of quality control procedures per the SOP, any problems or errors experienced during compounding, total quantity compounded, BUD assignment and storage requirements, and reference source of the BUD assignment and storage requirements.

- **Release Testing**

  - Before dispensing the NSC, it must be visually inspected to assess its physical appearance.
  - Must also confirm labeling accuracy from the original medication order.
  - Specific NSC must be inspected for specific characteristics, including emulsions for phase separation and pH assays.
  - Must be inspected if there is a delay from preparation to dispensing, including the container-closure system for leakage, cracks, or improper seals.

- **Labeling**

    - Assigned internal identification number (lot number)
    - Chemical/generic names, amounts, and concentrations
    - Dosage form
    - Total amount
    - Storage conditions
    - BUD
    - Identification of compounded preparation
    - Route of administration
    - Special handling instructions and warnings, when applicable
    - Name, address, and contact information for the compounding facility

- **Adverse Event Reporting**

    - Patients and prescribers should be informed, and the adverse event must be reviewed as part of a quality assurance and quality control program.
    - Report to the FDA MedWatch program for human drugs.
    - Report with Form FDA 1932a for veterinary drugs.

COMPOUNDING – USP 797 – STERILE COMPOUNDING

USP 797 describes the minimum standards when preparing compounded sterile human and animal drugs.

Core concepts include describing the aseptic technique for preparing any sterile medication and procedures to minimize the potential for contact with nonsterile surfaces.

United States Pharmacopeia (USP) 797

- **Sterile Compounding**

  - Admixing, combining, diluting, pooling, reconstituting, repackaging, or otherwise altering a drug product or bulk drug substance to create a sterile medication.
  - USP 797's overall objective is to minimize harm (from compounding errors to death) to human AND animal patients.
    - Other goals include reducing microbial contamination, excessive bacterial endotoxin production, variability from the intended strength of the right ingredients, physical and chemical incompatibilities, chemical and physical contamination, and the use of ingredients of inappropriate quality.
  - Pharmacists are the main profession performing sterile compounding, but it can be done by technicians, nurses, physicians, veterinarians, dentists, naturopaths, and chiropractors.
  - These regulations are not limited to injections, infusions, or parenteral medication compounds.
    - Includes irrigations for internal body cavities, ophthalmic dosage forms, preparations for pulmonary inhalation, baths and soaks for live organs and tissues, and implants.

- **General Practices**

  - Of note, USP has no role in enforcing these recommendations. Enforcement is up to the regulatory bodies (i.e., the State Board of Pharmacy).
  - All compounding areas must be certified using the Controlled Environment Testing Association (CETA) certification guide for sterile compounding facilities at least every 6 months.
    - Tests include airflow testing, HEPA filter integrity testing, total particle count testing, and dynamic airflow smoke pattern testing.
  - Repackaging is moving a sterile product from its original container into another container.
  - Hazardous drugs must meet all requirements for compounding under USP 797 and 800 (Hazardous Drugs Handling in Healthcare Settings).
  - Blood-derived and other biologic materials, including autologous serum, may be manipulated but must be separated from other compounding activities and equipment with separate standard operating procedures and follow additional jurisdictional standards.
  - Allergenic extracts are sterile and used for subcutaneous immunotherapy; they can be further diluted with an appropriate diluent for individual patients.
  - Sterile radiopharmaceuticals are beyond the scope of USP 797 and 800 but are regulated under USP 825 (Radiopharmaceuticals Preparation, Compounding, Dispensing, and Repackaging).

- **Hand Hygiene**

  - Must occur in the ante-room before entering the buffer room.
    - Ante-room is an International Standards Organization (ISO) Class 8 or cleaner room with fixed walls and doors acting as the transition room from the unclassified area to the buffer room.

- The buffer room is defined as an ISO Class 7 area where the primary engineering controls (PEC) that generate and maintain an ISO Class 5 environment are physically located.
- Professionals performing sterile compounding must not have nail polish, artificial nails, or makeup.
  - Other prohibitions include outer personal garments (jackets, sweatshirts, bandanas) and visible jewelry.
- Washing must be started by removing visible debris underneath fingernails under warm running water using a disposable nail pick or cleaner. Then, progress to hand washing up to the elbows with soap and water for at least 30 seconds. Dry completely from the hands to the elbows with lint-free disposable towels or wipers.
- Hand sanitization is different from the washing procedure.
  - Alcohol-based hand rubs must be applied to the dry skin of one hand, and then hands rubbed together to cover all surfaces, including fingernails until hands are completely dry before putting on sterile gloves.

- **Gowning**

  - Gown the dirtiest parts of the body to the cleanest.
    - Shoe covers, facial hair, hair, hands/nails, gown, gloves.
  - Gown is non-shedding, with cuffs around the wrists and enclosed at the neck.
    - Gowns can be removed and reused if stored in a nonhazardous compounding environment.
    - All other gowning components must be replaced.
  - Sterile gloves must be put on in a sterile environment and never used to touch any nonsterile surfaces.
    - Gloves must be sterilized using sterile 70% isopropyl alcohol and periodically re-sterilized during compounding activities after cleaning the laminar airflow workbench and if contamination is possible.

- **Hood Cleaning**

  - Clean from the cleanest parts to the dirtiest or most contaminated parts using lint-free wipes with sterile isopropyl alcohol.
    - The cleaning process is the reverse sequence compared to gowning.
    - The cleaning order depends on the hood type (horizontal vs. vertical).
      - Horizontal: Top of the hood, hanging pole, and any hooks, sides, bottom/work surface
      - Vertical: IV pole, back of the hood, sides, and work surface.
    - Use a new clean wipe for each new surface cleaned.
  - Cleaning should occur before beginning any compounding, every 30 minutes while compounding, immediately after any spill or contamination, and between different preparations.
  - Application of sporicidal agents must occur monthly in all locations.

- **Compounded Sterile Preparations (CSP) Categories**

  - CSP Category 1 compounds are assigned a beyond use date (BUD) $\leq$ 12 hours (at room temperature) or $\leq$ 24 hours (refrigerated).
  - CSP Category 2 compounds are assigned BUD > 12 hours (at room temperature) or > 24 hours (refrigerated).

- **Water Sources**

  - Sinks must be hands-free and equipped with surfaces cleaned and disinfected daily.
  - In a cleanroom suite, the sink must be used for hand hygiene inside or outside the ante-room area.

- For segregated compounding area (SCA) cleanrooms, the sink must be within 1 meter from the PEC and not located inside the perimeter of the SCA.

- **Primary Engineering Controls (PEC)**

  - The compounding area of a laminar flow hood is considered an ISO class 5 area.

  - Laminar airflow systems (LAFS) or hoods provide unidirectional airflow that produces purified air through high-efficiency particulate air (HEPA) filter.
    - HEPA air flow must never be blocked with the first airflow in contact with all critical sites.
      - Critical sites are the areas that, if touched, could lead to contamination of the final product, i.e., top of the vial, needle, or syringe plunger.
    - Biological Safety Cabinet (BSC) is a ventilated cabinet with an open front and inward/downward unidirectional HEPA-filtered airflow.
      - Provides worker protection from airborne drugs and ISO Class 5 or better environment.
    - Integrated vertical laminar flow zone (IVLFZ) provides an ISO Class 7 area with a physical barrier to direct airflow downward over the work area.
    - Vertical *negative* airflow pressure biological safety cabinets are the required environment for the sterile compounding of hazardous medications.
      - Flow should be continuous, and if turned off for any reason, it must be turned back on and run for 4 minutes before use.
    - Horizontal or vertical airflow pressure hoods are used for nonhazardous medications.
      - Flow should be continuous, and if turned off for any reason, it must be turned back on and run for at least 30 minutes before use.

  - Restricted-access barrier systems (RABS) are enclosed spaces with HEPA-filtered ISO Class 5 unidirectional air.
    - These devices include a compounding aseptic isolator (CAI) or compounding aseptic containment isolator (CACI).
    - Pharmaceutical isolators protect the surrounding area, maintaining ISO Class 5 air quality during dynamic operating conditions.
    - These include controlled workspace environments, transfer devices, access devices, and integral decontamination systems.

- **Secondary Engineering Controls (SEC)**

  - Facilities are physically designed and environmentally controlled to minimize airborne contamination.

  - ISO Classification and particle count
    - ISO class 3 – 35.2 /m^3
    - ISO class 4 – 352 /m^3
    - ISO class 5 – 3,520 /m^3
    - ISO class 6 – 35,200 /m^3
    - ISO class 7 – 352,000 /m^3
    - ISO class 8 – 3,520,000 /m^3

  - Ante-area is an ISO 7 or 8 area used for gowning and handwashing.

  - Buffer area is an ISO 7 area that is the main area where laminar flow hoods are located and requires a minimum of 30 air exchanges through the HEPA filter per hour.

- All items in the buffer area must be wiped and decontaminated before entering the buffer room.
- Floors and counters must be wiped daily.
- Walls, ceilings, shelves, and other items stored can be cleaned and wiped monthly.
- Low-risk compounded sterile products can also be compounded in this area but with no longer than a 12-hour beyond use date.

- **Segregated compounding area (SCA)**

  - PEC area should be located in an unclassified area without an ante-room or buffer room.
  - It cannot be located near unsealed windows, doors connected to the outside, and high-traffic areas.
  - Only category 1 CSPs can be compounded in these locations.

- **Compounded Sterile Product Risk Levels**

  - Immediate-use products are compounded in patient care areas.
    - Must also follow the requirements of low-risk CSP, aseptic techniques, and preparation that follows FDA-approved labeling standards.
    - Administration must occur within 4 hours from the start of preparation.

  - Low-Risk CSP – medication compounded in proper SEC environment and no ≤ 3 sterile medications with ≤ 2 entries into the containers.

  - Medium-risk CSP – a sterile medication from the manufacturer with compounding in an SEC with sterile equipment but has > 4 sterile medications with > 3 entries into containers.

  - High-risk CSP – any compound that involves a non-sterile component.

- **Master Formulation Records (MFR)**

  - Detailed report of procedures describing how CSPs are made.
  - Must include at least the following:
    - Name, strength or activity, and dosage form of the CSP
    - Identities and amounts of all ingredients.
    - Type and size of the container–closure system(s)
    - Complete instructions for preparing the CSP, including equipment, supplies, a description of the compounding steps, and any special precautions.
    - Physical description of the final CSP
    - BUD and storage requirements
    - Reference source to support the stability of the CSP
    - Quality control (QC) procedures
    - Other information to describe the compounding process and ensure repeatability.

- **Compounding Records**

  - Name, strength or activity, and dosage form of the CSP
  - Date and time of preparation of the CSP
  - Assigned internal identification number
  - A method to identify the individuals involved in the compounding process and verify the final CSP
  - Name of each component

- Vendor, lot number, and expiration date for each component for CSPs prepared for more than 1 patient, and CSPs prepared from nonsterile ingredients
- Weight or volume of each component
- Strength or activity of each component
- Total quantity compounded
- Assigned BUD and storage requirements
- Results of QC procedures
- MFR reference for the CSP
- Calculations made to determine and verify quantities and/or concentrations of the components

- **Labeling**

  - Assigned internal identification number (i.e., barcode, prescription, order, or lot number)
  - Active ingredient(s) and their amounts, activities, or concentrations
  - Storage conditions if other than controlled room temperature
  - BUD
  - Route of administration
  - Total amount or volume if it is not obvious from the container
  - If it is a single-dose container, a statement that indicates this when space permits
  - If it is a multiple-dose container, a statement stating this when space permits

- **Personnel Training**

  - Training on sterile technique is required for USP 797 regulation.
  - Content for training includes aseptic technique and proper procedures, with the trainees also performing numerous assessments before preparing CSPs for patients.
    - Core content for training and evaluation at least every 12 months includes hand hygiene, garbing, cleaning and disinfection, calculations, measuring and mixing, aseptic technique, achieving and/or maintaining sterility and pyrogenicity, use of equipment, documentation of the compounding, principles of HEPA-filtered unidirectional airflow within the ISO class 5 area, proper use of PECs, and principles of movement of materials and personnel within the compounding area.
  - Media fill testing is an annual assessment of the compounding individual's performance in preparing sterile products without contamination.

COMPOUNDING – USP 800 – HANDLING HAZARDOUS DRUGS

USP 800 contains the quality and practice standards for handling HD and promotes patient safety, worker safety, and environmental protection.

The general content outlines sterile and non-sterile HD's receipt, storage, compounding, dispensing, administration, and disposal.

United States Pharmacopeia (USP) 800 – Hazardous Drugs - Handling In Healthcare Settings

- **General Information**

  - Practice and quality standards for handling hazardous drugs (HDs) to promote patient safety, worker safety, and environmental protection.
    - HDs are categorized into 3 groups: antineoplastic drugs, nonantineoplastic drugs, and those nonantineoplastic drugs that mainly impact reproductive toxicity.
    - HDs display one of these criteria: carcinogenicity, teratogenicity, reproductive toxicity, genotoxicity, organ toxicity at low doses, and drugs that mimic existing drugs in structure or toxicity.

  - Includes receipt, storage, compounding, dispensing, administration, and disposal of sterile and nonsterile products and preparations and other information.

  - UPS 800 applies to all locations storing, preparing, transporting, or administering HDs.
    - Pharmacies, healthcare institutions, treatment clinics, physician practice facilities, or veterinarian offices

  - In addition to USP 800 recommendations, HD compounding must comply with USP 795 and 797, where applicable.

  - National Institute for Occupational Safety and Health (NIOSH) maintains the list of HDs in healthcare.
    - Any USP 800 facility must maintain this list and include all items on the NIOSH list and any additional item the facility deems necessary with a review every 12 months.

  - NIOSH containment requirements
    - Drugs on NIOSH list (HD, active pharmaceutical ingredient [API], antineoplastic requiring HD manipulation).
    - Certain drugs can be exempt from this NIOSH requirement if the compounded final dosage form does not require further manipulation other than counting or repackaging.

- **Types of Exposure**

  - Receipt of HD includes contacting HD residues on drug containers, individual dosage units, outer containers, work surfaces, or floors.

  - Exposure may occur at various times, including:
    - Crushing or splitting tablets or opening capsules
    - Pouring oral or topical liquids from one container to another
    - Weighing or mixing components
    - Constituting or reconstituting powdered or lyophilized HDs
    - Withdrawing or diluting injectable HDs from parenteral containers

- Expelling air or HDs from syringes
- Contacting HD residue present on PPE or other garments
- Deactivating, decontaminating, cleaning, and disinfecting areas contaminated with or suspected to be contaminated with HDs
- Maintenance activities for potentially contaminated equipment and devices
- Administration of HDs that generate aerosols by various routes, exposure during specialized procedures, or priming IV administration sites.
- Specialized procedures, including intraoperative intraperitoneal injections.
- Patient care activities include handling body fluids or fluid-contaminated clothing, dressings, linens, and other materials.
- Spills, transport, or HD wasting are potential exposure methods.

- **Handling HD**

    - A person(s) must be designated and qualified for developing and implementing appropriate procedures for handling HD.

    - Patient safety is key, and worker safety and environmental protection are considered.
        - Receipt of HDs and unpacking from external shipping containers must be done in a neutral/normal/negative pressure area to the surrounding area (i.e., not positive pressure).
        - HDs must be stored to minimize the container's spills, leaks, or breakage.

- **Compounding HD**

    - Engineering controls (primary, secondary, and supplemental levels of control) prevent cross-contamination and microbial contamination.

    - A containment primary engineering control (C-PEC) is a ventilated device to minimize worker and environmental HD exposure.
        - Buffer rooms that house C-PEC must be externally vented or have a redundant HEPA filter system.
        - For sterile compounding, it must have an ISO Class 5 or better air quality.

    - Containment secondary engineering control (C-SEC) is the room where the C-PEC is placed.
        - Must be externally vented, physically separated from other preparation areas, and have an appropriate air exchange and a negative pressure between 0.01 and 0.03 inches of water column relative to all adjacent areas.
        - ISO Class 7 buffer room and ante-room
        - Must have a sink for hand washing, an eyewash station, and other emergency precaution areas in the ante-room at least 1 meter from the entrance.

    - Supplementary engineering controls (including closed-system drug transfer devices [CSTD]) are additional controls that offer more levels of protection.

    - Unlike USP 797 environments, a laminar airflow workbench (LAFW) or a compounding aseptic isolator (CAI) cannot be used for compounding antineoplastic HDs.

- **Environmental Quality and Control**

    - HD surface environmental wipe sampling must occur initially and at least every 6 months.
    - However, there is no standard for acceptable limits for HD surface contamination.
        - Common marker HDs are assessed (i.e., cyclophosphamide, ifosfamide, methotrexate, fluorouracil, and platinum-containing drugs).

- Studies have demonstrated drug exposure to workers after HD manipulation.

- **Personal Protective Equipment (PPE)**

    - For worker safety and protection, PPE is required to handle HDs outside C-PEC areas.
        - PPE cannot be reused, as in USP 797.

    - Appropriate PPE during HD handling includes gowns, head, hair, and shoe covers, and two chemotherapy gloves.
        - Must be worn when handling HD, including during receipt, storage, transport, compounding, administration, deactivation/decontamination, cleaning, disinfecting, spill control, and waste disposal.

    - Gloves must meet American Society for Testing and Materials (ASTM) standard D6978.
        - Chemotherapy-specific, powder-free gloves must be worn when handling all HD medications (including non-antineoplastics), inspected before use, and changed every 30 minutes (or when torn, punctured, or contaminated).
        - Hands must be washed before AND after removing gloves.

    - Gowns are specific to the HD being handled, must close in the back, be long-sleeved, and have closed cuffs.
        - Cloth laboratory coats, surgical scrubs, isolation gowns, or similar apparel are insufficient for protective outerwear.
        - Gowns must be changed per the manufacturer's recommendation every 2-3 hours or immediately after a spill or splash.

    - Head, hair, shoe, and sleeve covers are required when compounding HD.
        - Double shoe covers are required before entering any C-SEC and removed when exiting the C-SEC.

    - Appropriate eye and face protection must be worn when specific risks for spills or splashes of HD or HD waste products exist during work outside the C-PEC.
        - Normal eyeglasses alone are insufficient eye protection, so goggles are required.

    - Respiratory protection using an elastomeric half-mask with a multi-gas cartridge and P100-filter are needed for individuals unpacking HD that are not contained in plastic to avoid exposure after breakage or spillage.
        - N95 surgical respirators are adequate respiratory protection but do not offer protection against gases and vapors and offer little protection against direct liquid splashes.

- **Hazard Communication Program**

    - Standard operating procedures (SOP) for effective training in labeling, transport, storage, and disposal of HDs are required.

    - Required components of the hazard communication program
        - A written plan describes how the standard will be implemented.
        - All containers of hazardous chemicals must be labeled, tagged, or marked with the identity of the material and appropriate hazard warnings.
        - Entities must have a Safety Data Sheet (SDS) for each hazardous chemical they use.
        - Entities must ensure that the SDSs for each hazardous chemical used are readily accessible to personnel during each work shift and in their work areas.

- Personnel who may be exposed to hazardous chemicals when working must be provided with information and training before the initial assignment to work with a hazardous chemical and whenever the hazard changes.
- Personnel of reproductive capability must confirm in writing that they understand the risks of handling HDs.

- **Personnel Training**

  - Core components must include at least the following:
    - Overview of the entity's list of HDs and their risks
    - Review of the entity's SOPs related to the handling of HDs
    - Proper use of PPE
    - Proper use of equipment and devices (i.e., engineering controls)
    - Response to known or suspected HD exposure
    - Spill management
    - Proper disposal of HDs and trace-contaminated material

- **Receiving HDs**

  - If the shipping container appears damaged, the container must be sealed without opening, and the supplier must be immediately contacted.
    - If the unopened package is returned to the supplier, enclose the package in a new impervious container labeled "Hazardous."
    - If the supplier declines the return, the HD must be disposed of as hazardous waste.

  - If a damaged shipping container must be opened, the container must be sealed in plastic or an impervious container, transported to a C-PEC, and placed on a plastic-backed preparation mat. Once there, the package can be opened, and the undamaged items removed and wiped.
    - The damaged item(s) must be enclosed in an impervious waste container labeled "Hazardous."
      - The C-PEC must then be deactivated, decontaminated, and cleaned of hazardous waste.
        - Deactivation renders the compound inert or inactive (i.e., peroxide formulations or sodium hypochlorite)
        - Decontamination is the removal of HD residue (i.e., alcohol, water, peroxide, or sodium hypochlorite)
        - Cleaning removes organic and inorganic material using a germicidal detergent.
    - If the supplier declines to return, the HD must be disposed of as hazardous waste.

- **Labeling, Packaging, Transport, Disposal**

  - HDs may require special HD handling precautions defined by the manufacturer and must be clearly labeled during transport.
  - Packaging materials must maintain the HD's physical integrity, stability, and sterility (if necessary) during transport.
  - The HD must be labeled, stored, and handled appropriately according to federal, state, or local regulations during transportation.
  - Disposal must occur in HD handling areas by trained individuals and according to federal, state, or local regulations.

- **Compounding**

  - When compounded in a C-PEC, a plastic-backed preparation mat should be placed on the work surface that can be changed immediately for a spill and regularly during use.

- **Administration**

  - Appropriate PPE must be worn when the administration of HDs occurs and disposed of in waste-approved containers after administration.
  - A healthcare professional must not manipulate HD dosage forms for administration (i.e., crushing tablets, opening capsules).

- **Spill Control**

  - Personnel cleaning an HD spill must undergo proper training in spill management and use PPE and NIOSH-certified respirators.
  - Spills must be contained and cleaned immediately, with appropriate personnel always available.
  - Spill kits with the proper materials must be readily available.
  - Signs must be posted for restricted access to the spill area.

- **Medical Surveillance**

  - Healthcare workers handling HD must be enrolled in a medical surveillance program to minimize the adverse health effects of HD exposure.
  - May assist in identifying weaknesses in procedures, engineering controls, or training programs.
  - Components of medical surveillance programs include assessment and documentation of symptom complaints, physical findings, and laboratory values to determine risks outside of established normal exposures.
  - Examines individuals and populations of healthcare workers who handle HDs and must be consistent with the entity's Human Resource policy.
    - Must have an organized approach to identify potentially exposed workers based on their job description.
  - Medical records of surveillance should be maintained according to OSHA regulations.
  - Should protect the confidentiality of the employees' personal medical information.
  - Surveillance programs should include a range of content:
    - Initial baseline assessment of health status and medical history.
      - Reproductive history and work history to assess the effects of exposure to HDs
      - Physical examination and laboratory testing related to target organs affected by commonly used HDs.
      - Records of HDs handled, with quantities and dosage forms
      - Estimated number of HDs handled per week
      - Estimate of hours spent handling HDs per week and/or per month
      - Performance of a physical assessment and laboratory studies linked to target organs of commonly used HDs
      - Monitoring of the data to identify where prevention failure has occurred, leading to health effects
      - Development of a follow-up plan for workers who have shown health changes suggesting toxicity or have experienced acute exposure
      - Completion of an exit examination

- **Follow-Up Plan**

    - Occurs after an exposure-related health change and immediate re-evaluation of primary preventative measures in place.
    - Perform a post-exposure examination tailored to the type of exposure.
    - Treatment and laboratory studies will follow as indicated and be guided by emergency protocols.
    - Compare the performance of controls with recommended standards and conduct environmental sampling when analytical methods are available.
    - Verify and document that all engineering controls are in proper operating condition.
    - Verify and document that the worker complied with existing policies.
    - Develop and document a plan of action that will prevent additional exposure of workers.
    - Ensure confidential, two-way communication between the worker and the employee health unit(s).
    - Provide and document a follow-up medical survey to demonstrate that the plan implemented is effective.
    - Ensure that any exposed worker receives confidential notification of adverse health effects. Offer alternative duty or temporary reassignment.
    - Provide ongoing medical surveillance of all workers at risk for exposure to HDs to determine whether the plan implemented is effective.

COMPOUNDING – USP 825 - RADIOPHARMACEUTICALS

USP 825 specifically outlines the handling of radiopharmaceuticals.

Provides uniform minimum standards for preparing, compounding, dispensing, and repackaging sterile and nonsterile radiopharmaceuticals for humans and animals.

These regulations apply to all radiopharmaceutical processing activities and sterile intravascular radioactive devices.

United States Pharmacopeia (USP) 825 – Radiopharmaceuticals – Preparation, Compounding, Dispensing, and Repackaging

- **General Information**

    - Radioactive materials (RAMs) fall under the control of the US Nuclear Regulatory Commission (NRC) or NRC-contracted agreement state agencies.
        - Other federal regulatory authorities, including the FDA and the Department of Transportation, have control over RAMs.

    - Applies to all individuals and practice settings where radiopharmaceuticals are prepared, compounded, dispensed, or repackaged.
        - Practice settings include state-licensed nuclear pharmacies, federal nuclear pharmacy facilities, nuclear medicine departments in hospitals or clinics, nuclear cardiology clinics, and other specialty clinics.
        - Personnel includes authorized nuclear pharmacists (ANP), authorized user (AU) physicians, and individuals working under their supervision (student pharmacists, nuclear pharmacy technicians, physician residents and trainees, and nuclear medicine technologists and students).

    - Radiopharmaceuticals exist as nonsterile and sterile agents.
        - Nonsterile agents include oral capsules or solutions.
        - Sterile radiopharmaceuticals can be injectables, inhalations, and ophthalmics.

- **Radiation Safety**

    - Safe handling of radiopharmaceuticals requires precautions to be followed that are set by special radiation regulatory authorities.
        - An example is the as low as reasonably achievable (ALARA) practice.

    - Aseptic handling practices must be balanced with radiation safety considerations.
        - This is determined through knowledge, experience, and professional judgment related to the type, abundance, and energy of the radioactive emissions, the quantity of radioactivity, and other factors that vary depending on the case.

    - The inverse square law is a determination of radiation exposure. In other words, increasing distance decreases radiation exposure.

    - Shielding materials, including lead or tungsten in various configurations, protect from radiation exposure to personnel.
        - L-block, torso, vial, and syringe shields are required throughout the radiopharmaceutical handling process in an ISO Class 5 primary engineering control (PEC).

- Radioactive material (RAM) contamination from spills, drips, sprays, volatility, or other means warrants radiation protection.
    - Methods for radiation protection include vial contents being maintained at neutral or negative pressure, disposable absorbent pads, vertical airflow in PEC, and needleless systems.

- Suitable radiation measuring devices like dose calibrators are needed as radiation detectors during radiopharmaceutical handling and can be placed inside an ISO Class 5 PEC.

- Individuals must wear body and extremity dosimeters for long-term monitoring of personnel radiation exposure.
    - The dosimeter should be worn underneath the gown, and the extremity dosimeter should be worn underneath properly fitting gloves without interference.

- **Personnel**

    - Appropriate qualifications for radiopharmaceutical work must be documented and comply with the policies/procedures of the authorized nuclear pharmacists (ANP) or authorized users (AU).
        - Any personnel with rashes, sunburns, recent tattoos, oozing sores, conjunctivitis, or active respiratory infections must report these to their supervisor, who will determine if the individual is excluded from working in sterile processing areas.

    - Content for training includes aseptic technique and proper procedures, with the trainees also performing numerous assessments before preparing radiopharmaceuticals.
        - Core content for training and evaluation at least every 6 months includes hand hygiene, garbing, cleaning and disinfection, calculations, measuring and mixing, aseptic technique, achieving and/or maintaining sterility and pyrogenicity, use of equipment, documentation of compounding, principles of HEPA-filtered unidirectional airflow within the ISO class 5 area, proper use of PECs, and principles of movement of materials and personnel within the compounding area.

    - Media fill testing is an annual assessment of the compounding individual's performance in preparing sterile products without contamination.
        - Glove fingertip and thumb sampling are also required to demonstrate aseptic manipulation and cleaning competency.

- **Hand Hygiene**

    - Must occur when radiopharmaceuticals are repackaged, dispensed, and prepared in an ISO Class 5 PEC.

    - The segregated radiopharmaceutical processing area (SRPA) is a specific classification of a buffer room.
        - Before entering, SRPA personnel must remove outer garments, cosmetics, visible personal garments (jackets, sweatshirts, bandanas), and jewelry.
        - Radiation dosimetry devices are allowed.

    - Hand washing must be done before entering the SRPA.
        - Remove visible debris underneath fingernails under warm running water using a disposable nail cleaner and nail pick.
        - Progress to hand washing up to the elbows with soap and water for at least 30 seconds.
        - Dry the hands to the elbows completely with low-lint disposable towels or wipers.

    - Hand sanitization is different from the washing procedure.

- Alcohol-based hand rubs must be applied to the dry skin of one hand; then, hands rubbed together to cover all surfaces, including fingernails, until hands are entirely dry before putting on sterile gloves.

— When exiting the SRPA, the exterior gown and wall coverings must be properly disposed of, with all new garments donned before re-entry.
   — Unlike USP 797, gowns cannot be re-used.

- **Facility Controls and Engineering Controls**

— General cleaning, control, and maintenance requirements follow USP 795 or 797 requirements.

— Radiopharmaceutical facilities must have a well-lit and comfortable working environment (temperature of 25°C or cooler, humidity below 60%) that is evaluated every 12 months.

— All surfaces (i.e., ceilings, walls, floors, doors, fixtures, work surfaces, etc.) in classified rooms (PEC, SRPA, SEC) must be smooth, impervious, free from cracks, and non-shedding to facilitate easy cleaning.
   — Certification of classified areas in the PEC must be done initially and for recertification (every 6 months) using procedures in the Controlled Environment Testing Association (CETA) certification guide.
   — Cleaning of these areas must be scheduled using cleaning agents, disinfecting agents, and sporicidal agents.

— RAM licenses must comply with negative pressure obligations.
   — Buffer room must be positive pressure compared to the ante-room.
   — Ante-room must be positive pressure compared to a restricted area.
   — The restricted area must be negative pressure to the open area.
   — SRPA must be negative pressure to unrestricted areas in the presence of volatile or airborne radiopharmaceuticals.

— Secondary engineering control (SEC) areas house PECs, which can be either a buffer room with an ante-room or an SRPA.
   — SRPAs are areas with PECs within an unclassified room without an ante-room.
      — Must include an ISO Class 5 PEC (vertical laminar airflow workbench or Class II Biological Safety Cabinet.
         — May not include a glove box, which is a negative pressure radiological container without a HEPA filter.
      — Only sterile radiopharmaceutical preparation, preparation with minor deviations, dispensing, and repackaging may be performed in these locations.
      — Must also be located away from unsealed windows, doors connecting to the outside, and traffic flow which may adversely affect the quality of the PEC.
   — SRPAs cannot be located adjacent to environmental control challenges (such as bathrooms).

— Materials should move from lower to higher quality rooms, i.e., moving from ISO Class 8 ante-room areas to ISO Class 7 buffer rooms to ISO Class 5 PEC.

— Air sampling of all classified spaces using an impaction device must be conducted during dynamic operating conditions every 6 months.

- The process for required testing should follow the manufacturer's instructions, test at least 1000 L of air from each location sampled, incubate the media, and assess for microbial growth.

- **Radiopharmaceutical Processing Environment**

  - PEC area must qualify as an ISO Class 5 or better to minimize the potential for microbial contamination.
    - Laminar airflow is required due to the particle collection efficiency of the filter.
    - HEPA-filtered air must supply critical areas, such ISO-Class 5 areas, at a velocity sufficient to sweep particles away from aseptic processing areas and prevent turbulence and stagnant air in critical areas.

  - HEPA-filtered air maintained in ISO classification areas is measured by air changes per hour (ACPH).
    - ACPH requirement is higher depending on the ISO classification, the number of personnel in the work area, the number of particulates generated from activities and processes in the area, equipment in the room, room pressure, and the effects of temperature.
    - ISO Class 7 areas require a minimum of 30 total HEPA-filtered ACPH.
      - Other requirements include > 15 ACPH of total air from HVAC through HEPA filters in the ceiling.
    - ISO Class 8 areas require > 20 ACPH of HEPA-filtered air from the HVAC through the HEPA filters in the ceiling.
    - Unclassified SRPA areas do not have a specific ACPH requirement.

  - Hot-cell devices provide physical segregation for ISO Class 5 aseptic processing areas.

- **Beyond Use Date (BUD)**

  - BUD is determined from the risk of microbial contamination, assuming the radiopharmaceutical remains chemically and physically stable.
    - Other considerations for BUD include the maintenance of appropriate quality and purity, including radiochemical purity, radionuclidic purity, and other applicable parameters.
  - The time starts with the puncture of the first vial.
  - Elements that affect the BUD are wide-ranging, including sterility, radiochemical purity, radionuclidic purity, generator age, number of particles, specific activity or molar mass, and container type.

- **Master Formulation Record (MFR)**

  - Required if prepared with minor deviations (i.e., not required for preparation following manufacturer's instructions).
  - Records for preparation with minor deviation in compounding must include the name of the radiopharmaceutical, physical description of the final radiopharmaceutical (dosage form), name and quantity of ingredients, including calibration time for radioactive ingredients, total volume, reference to the MFR, any deviation from the MFR, name of vendor or manufacturer, lot number, and expiration date of all ingredients, name of the person preparing and supervising personnel, date and time of preparation, internal ID number, prescription or order number, assigned BUD, storage requirements, PEC documentation of quality control results, and reference source of the BUD.
  - Examples of minor deviations include using test methods other than those in the product labeling or filtering Tc-99m sulfur colloid.

- **Preparation of Radiolabeled Blood Components**

    - Blood component handling and radiolabeling require universal precautions and aseptic technique and must be administered within 6 hours after labeling.
    - ISO Class 5 BSC must be in an ISO Class 7 buffer room for blood labeling.
    - Personnel working in one PEC can only work with one labeling procedure per PEC at a time.
        - Blood products for more than one patient can never be in the same workstation simultaneously and must be completely separated to prevent cross-contamination.
    - Replace any garb that entered the ISO Class 5 environment before handling anything unrelated to the given blood procedure.

- **Compounding**

    - Must be based on pre-established written procedures and include maintenance of compounding records.
    - Nonsterile compounding occurs if materials are combined, mixed, diluted, pooled, reconstituted, or otherwise altered outside information provided in the package insert.
        - Nonsterile radiopharmaceutical compounding must occur in a location separate from those intended for sterile radiopharmaceuticals.
    - Sterile compounding is completed with aseptic technique in an ISO Class 5 environment.
        - May involve using materials other than commercially available products.
        - Identity, quality, and purity testing must be performed before dispensing to use these products.

- **Dispensing**

    - Except for the unopened manufacturer container, the final patient dose or ordered amount must be radioassayed in a dose calibrator and mathematically corrected for radioactive decay to the time of scheduled administration.

- **Labeling**

    - Numerous requirements exist for labeling radiopharmaceuticals and largely depend on the specific state board of pharmacy.
    - General requirements for inner container labeling include:
        - Standard radiation symbol
        - "Caution-Radioactive Material" label
        - Patient name/identifier for all therapeutic and blood products
        - Radionuclide and chemical form (generic name)
        - Radioactivity with units at the time of calibration and the calibration time
    - Outer shielding labeling requirements include:
        - Standard radiation symbol
        - "Caution-Radioactive Material" label
        - Patient name/identifier for all therapeutic and blood products
        - Calibration date and time for the dose
        - Activity dispensed with units at calibration date and time
        - Radionuclide and chemical form
        - Volume dispensed
        - Number of dosage units dispensed
        - BUD

- **Repackaging**

    - Removing an FDA-approved radiopharmaceutical from its original container to place it into a different container without any product manipulation.
        - Also includes placing contents of multiple containers of the same finished product into one container that does not include other ingredients.

    - Can be done for both nonsterile and sterile radiopharmaceuticals.

CALCULATIONS – BASIC PRINCIPLES

1. **Unit conversions**

   a. Imperial
      i. Weight (Pound, ounce, dram, scruple, grain)
      ii. Volume (gallon, quart, pint, fluid ounce, fluid dram, minim)
   b. Metric (International System of Units)
      i. Weight
      ii. Volume
   c. Household System
      i. Tablespoon, teaspoon, cup
   d. Temperature
      i. Fahrenheit, Celsius, Kelvin

2. **Abbreviations and Related Numbers**

   a. ss = 0.5
   b. I = 1
   c. V = 5
   d. X = 10
   e. L = 50
   f. C = 100
   g. D = 500
   h. M = 1000

3. **Percent and Ratio**

   a. W/W = grams of ingredient in 100 grams of the product; assumed for mixtures of solids and semisolids
   b. V/V = milliliters of ingredient in 100 milliliters of the product; assumed for solutions of liquids in liquids
   c. W/V = grams of ingredient in 100 milliliters of the product; assumed for solutions or suspensions of solids in liquids or gases in liquids

All healthcare professionals play a fundamental role in safely and effectively using medications.

- **Knowledge must extend beyond drug information.**

    - Must include skills required to transform medication into appropriate dosage forms for administration.

- **Specific pharmaceutical skills must include the following:**

    - Calculating individual drug doses.
    - Accurate conversion between units of measurement.

- **Using dimensional analysis and ratio-proportion calculation methods is how drugs are dispensed at appropriate doses for each patient.**

CALCULATIONS – UNITS OF MEASURE

Units of Measure

- Without units of measure, numbers and digits in a formula would be meaningless to practical application.

- Four systems of measure:

    - **Apothecaries' system**

        - Still found in modern pharmaceutical applications
        - Employs **minims** for liquids and **grains** for solids
            - Ex: phenobarbital, which can be ordered or prescribed in grains
        - Volume = 1 pint is equivalent to 16 fluid ounces
        - Weight = pounds (lb), ounces (oz)

    - **Avoirdupois system**

        - With this system, 1 lb is 16 oz (versus 1 lb = 12 oz in the apothecary system).

    - **International System of Units (SI), formerly known as the metric system**

        - The most logical system to recognize as each unit of measure is a factor or power of 10
            - For example, the decimal is moved three spaces when converting from a milliliter to a liter, i.e., 1000 mL of normal saline is equivalent to 1 L of normal saline.

    - **Household system**

        - Commonly used measurement system
        - Teaspoons, tablespoons, cups, pints, quarts, and gallons describe volume.

Apothecary – Weight

Pound (lb.)	Ounce (oz)	Dram	Scruple	Grain
1	12	96	288	5760
	1	8	24	480
		1	3	60
			1	20
				1

Apothecary – Volume

Gallon (gal)	Quart (qt)	Pint (pt)	Fluid Ounce (fl oz)	Fluid Dram	Minim
1	4	8	128	1024	61440
	1	2	32	256	15360
		1	16	128	7680
			1	8	480
				1	60

Avoirdupois

Pound (lb)	Ounce (oz)	Grain (gr)
1	16	7000
	1	437.5

Temperature

- Fahrenheit, Celsius, and Kelvin

  - Describing the difference between these units, using water's freezing and boiling points, can help provide context.
  - Water freezes at zero degrees Celsius, 32 degrees Fahrenheit, and 273 degrees Kelvin.
  - Water boils at 100-degree degrees Celsius, 212 degrees Fahrenheit, and 273 degrees Kelvin 373.1 Kelvin.
  - Fever in Fahrenheit is 100.4 degrees, which is 38 degrees Celsius.

Number Systems

- Calculations are accomplished using two numbering systems:

  - Arabic
  - Roman Numerals

Roman Numeral	Meaning
ss	0.5
I or i	1
V or v	5
X or x	10
L or l	50
C or c	100
D or d	500
M or m	1000

- **Roman**

  - Written prescriptions frequently contain a Roman numeral representation of the desired quantity of a given dosage form.
    - For example, the prescription sig "i tab PO daily" instructs the dispensing pharmacist to dispense a sufficient quantity to give the patient one tablet by mouth daily.

  - When Roman numerals are grouped, they are interpreted using addition or subtraction.
    - Super Bowl LI, or Super Bowl 51, where L = 50 and I = 1 are added together.
    - A prescription may call for 150 mL written as CL, which equals 100 + 50.
    - For prescriptions with a quantity of IV tablets, subtraction is necessary (5 minus 1 = 4).

- **Arabic**

  - Often referred to as the decimal system
  - The decimal acts as an anchor.
  - Each place to the left of the decimal identifies an increase of 10x, whereas each place to the right denotes a 10x decrease.

Percent and Ratio

- When administered, a given medication's dosage form likely contains active and inactive ingredients.

- To appropriately describe the amount of each active ingredient, there are several methods to select from:

1. **Percent**
   a. Describes the number of a given part per 100 parts.
      i. W/W describes the grams of ingredients in 100 grams of the product.
         1. Assumed for mixtures of solids and semisolids (g/100 g)
      ii. V/V describes milliliters of ingredients in 100 milliliters of the product.
         1. Assumed for solutions of liquids in liquids (mL/100 mL)
      iii. W/V describes grams of ingredients in 100 milliliters of the product.
         1. Assumed for solutions or suspensions of solids in liquids or gases in liquids (g/100 mL)

   b. The percentages representing these measures can be written or expressed as decimals or using the percent symbol (%).
      i. Converting from the decimal digit to % requires dividing or multiplying by 100, depending on the conversion.
         1. For example, lidocaine 2% can also be represented as lidocaine 2 g/100mL.
            a. 2g/100mL x 1000 mg/1g = 2000 mg/100mL (canceling two zeros in the numerator 2000 and two zeros in the denominator 100), we get 20 mg/mL
            b. So now, to give 100 mg, we arrange the following calculation: 100 mg / x mL = 20 mg / 1 mL; rearranging to solve for "x," we know that x = 1 mL x 100 mg / 20 mg; x = 5 mL

2. **Ratio strength**
   a. How much epinephrine in milligrams would a patient receive from a 0.5 mL epinephrine 1:1000 intramuscular injection?
      i. A 1:1000 ratio can be expressed as 1 part epinephrine per 1,000 parts of solution; in other words, 0.1 parts epinephrine per 100 parts solution can be represented using a percentage proportion described above (W/V%) where there is 0.1 g of epinephrine per 100 mL solution.
         1. 0.1 g / 100 mL x 1000 mg / 1 g = 100 mg / 100 mL; Canceling two zeros in the numerator and denominator, we know that 1 mg of epinephrine is in 1 mL solution.
         2. X g / 0.5 mL = 1 mg / 1 mL, where X g = 0.5 mL x 1 mg / 1 mL = 0.5 mL

3. **Parts per million, parts per billion, or parts per trillion**
   a. Parts per million (ppm), parts per billion (ppb), or parts per trillion (ppt) are unique cases of ratio strength used to describe very dilute concentrations.
      i. Few medications and doses use ppm, ppb, or ppt, but occupational exposures to potentially toxic substances are frequently described using these measures.
         1. According to OSHA, the permissible exposure limit (PEL) to ammonia in the workplace is 50 ppm, whereas the potentially dangerous threshold is 300 ppm.
         2. We could express this ppm as 50 parts per 1,000,000 parts of the solution.

CALCULATIONS – ALLIGATION, MILLIEQUIVALENTS, & MILLIOSMOLES

Preparation of solutions (Dilution, concentration, powder volume, and alligation)

- Concentration

  - Concentration is the quantity of solute divided by the quantity of the preparation. Some examples include:
    - Normal saline, a 0.9% sodium chloride solution, means there are 0.9 parts of the drug in 100 parts of the solution. In this case (recalling W/V), 0.9 g of the drug is in 100 mL of the solution.
    - A ratio can also describe the solution, as in epinephrine 1:1000, where there is 1 part per 1000 parts solution or 1 g in 1000 mL (otherwise described as 1mg / 1mL).

- **Dilution**

  - Dilution refers to adding volume to a given drug to reduce its concentration.
    - Intravenous potassium chloride is commercially available as a 2 mEq/mL solution.
      - This is far too concentrated for safe administration to any patient and requires further dilution.
      - To achieve the desired final concentration of 20 mEq / 100 mL normal saline, how much potassium chloride 2 mEq/mL should be added to the 100 mL normal saline bag?
        - X mL / 20 mEq = 1 mL / 2 mEq
        - X mL = 20 mEq x 1 mL / 2 mEq
        - X = 10 mL
        - For this desired final concentration of 20 mEq / 100 mL normal saline, you must dilute 10 mL of potassium chloride 2 mEq/mL in 100 mL normal saline.

- **Powder Volume**

  - A 21-year-old patient is treated for a sexually transmitted disease (Neisseria gonorrhoeae) with ceftriaxone 500 mg administered as a single intramuscular injection. The reconstitution instructions state that you are to add 1.0 mL of sterile water to the 500 mg vial, yielding a final concentration of 350 mg/mL (note that the concentration changed!). To give the prescribed dose of 500 mg, what is the volume of ceftriaxone solution to be administered?

    - x mL / 500 mg = 1 mL / 350 mg
    - x mL = 500 mg x 1 mL / 350 mg = 1.4 mL.
      - In this case, we add 1.0 mL but can withdraw 1.4 mL! This is a result of the volume taken by the powdered drug itself.
      - This consideration does not necessarily need to be accounted for with each drug in a powdered form, but careful analysis of the prescribing information is required to determine when to do this.

- **Alligation**

    - Alligation is the mixing of solutions or solids possessing different percentages of strengths to get a given final concentration or percentage strength.
        - Alligation involves changing the percentages to parts and using ratio and proportion to solve each initial product's unknown amount.
            - A patient suffered a traumatic brain injury from a gunshot to the head. Before attempting a neurosurgical intervention, their initial resuscitation requires a hypertonic sodium chloride infusion to reduce intracranial pressure.
            - The neurosurgeon orders an infusion of 100 mL of sodium chloride 7.5%.
                - You rapidly recognize that you do not carry a commercially available product with that concentration, and one must be prepared.
                - In searching for options, you find one vial of 23.4% sodium chloride and an intravenous bag of 3% sodium chloride.
                - How much of each is required to make 100 mL of 7.5% sodium chloride?
        - The first step to solving this problem requires subtracting the final target concentration from the larger starting concentration and subtracting the lesser concentration from the final target concentration. Set up this classic "X" pattern relationship for alligation.

    - Based on the above calculation, we require 4.5 "parts" of 23.4% sodium chloride and 15.9 "parts" of sodium chloride 3%.
    - Adding the two together, 20.4 parts is the final total parts. To determine the actual volumes to make approximately 100 mL (final volume), we can make the following calculations:
        1. 100 mL / 20.4 parts = X mL 23.4% sodium chloride / 4.5 parts
            - X mL 23.4% sodium chloride = 100 mL x 4.5 parts / 20.4 parts
            - X = 22.05 mL 23.4% sodium chloride
        2. 100 mL / 20.4 parts = X mL 3% sodium chloride / 15.9 parts
            - X mL 3% sodium chloride = 100 mL x 15.9 parts / 20.4 parts
            - X = 79.1 mL 3% sodium chloride
        3. Therefore, we must add 22.05 mL of 23.4% sodium chloride to 79.1 mL of 3% sodium chloride to make the final desired concentration of 7.5%, with a volume of 101.15 (within a 10% acceptable range).

Density

- Density is the relationship between the mass of a substance and the volume it occupies (D= mass/volume)

    - Density calculations convert a given weight to a volume (or volume to weight).
    - The typical units to describe density are mass units over volume units, i.e., g/mL.

Specific gravity

- Specific gravity is a similar description of a given medication's weight ratio to the same volume of standard material (water is often the standard material for liquids).

    - No units describe specific gravity since mathematics cancels out the units used in its calculation.
    - Specific gravity = weight of a substance/weight of an equal volume of water

Milliequivalent

- Milliequivalent (mEq) is a unit measuring an electrolyte's chemical activity according to its valence.
- It also refers to an inorganic molecule's dissociation ability in a liquid.
- mEq is used routinely to describe the quantity or dose of many electrolytes, such as potassium chloride.
- To convert the provided dose to milligrams or milliequivalents, the following equation can be used:

    - mEq = mg element x valence / molecular weight
    - In the case of calcium, which has a molecular weight of 40.078 and a valence of 2, we can determine the dose in mEq from 500 mg of calcium.
        - mEq = 500 mg x 2 / 40.078
        - mEq = 24.95 mEq

Moles and Millimoles

- The mole measurement is the molecular weight of a substance in grams.
- Millimole is the same weight as milligram.

    - Avogadro's number is the number of particles in 1 mole (or 1 gram of molecular weight) per liter of solution.
    - Ex: You need to determine the weight of 5 moles of calcium (Calcium atomic weight = 40.078 g).
        - 1 mole of calcium = 40.078 g (atomic weight)
        - 5 moles = 40.078 g (atomic weight in g) x 5
        - 5 moles = 200.39 g

Milliosmoles

- Going back to the previous alligation example where a patient required sodium chloride 7.5%, we would have to go one step further to ensure it can be safely administered.

- The osmotic concentration would need to be determined to see if the drug can be given through a peripheral IV (limit of 900 mOsmol/L) or if it requires a central IV due to the risk of serious harm with extravasation.

  - This osmotic concentration is the total number of particles in the solution and is expressed in milliosmoles (mOsmol).
    - mOsmol/L = weight of a substance (g/L) x number of species x 1000 / molecular weight (g)
    - Sodium chloride 7.5% = 7.5 g / 100 mL or 75g / 1L
    - Number of species for NaCl = 2
    - The molecular weight of Na = 22.9 g
    - The molecular weight of Cl = 35.45 g
    - mOsmol/L = 75 g/L x 2 x 1000 / (22.9 + 35.45)
    - mOsmol/L = 2566.7 mOsmol/L
    - Therefore, NaCl 7.5%'s osmolarity is hypertonic at 2566.7 mOsmol/L and should be administered via central IV.

CALCULATIONS – RECONSTITUTION & IV INFUSION RATES

Reconstitution and IV Infusion Rates

- **A 21-year-old patient is treated for a sexually transmitted disease (Neisseria gonorrhoeae) with ceftriaxone 500 mg administered as a single intramuscular injection.**

  - The reconstitution instructions state that you are to add 1.0 mL of sterile water to the 500 mg vial, yielding a final concentration of 350 mg/mL (note that the concentration changed!).
  - To give the prescribed dose of 500 mg, what is the volume of ceftriaxone solution to be administered?
    - Arranging the proportion relationship:
      - x mL / 500 mg = 1 mL / 350 mg
      - Solving for x, x mL = 500 mg x 1 mL / 350 mg = 1.4 mL.

- **In practice, you could not quickly and accurately measure 1.42857143 mL.**

  - Using a 3mL syringe, the sensitivity is only to a single decimal point, so we must round up or down, following the principles of rounding rules:
    - If the digit to be eliminated is less than 5, round down to eliminate it by changing the preceding digit (i.e., 4.54 to 4.5).
    - If the digit to be eliminated is 5 or greater, round up by increasing the preceding digit by 1 (i.e., 4.55 to 4.6).
  - Round at the end of multiple-step calculations, not at the beginning or in the middle.
  - Knowing how many decimals to include depends on the clinical scenario.

- **Reconstruction of Crotalidae polyvalent immune fab (CroFab).**

  - For the initial treatment of a North American Pit Viper envenomation, the dose is 4 vials diluted in a final volume of 250 mL normal saline and administered over 1 hour.
    - First, reconstitute each vial with 18 mL of normal saline, yielding a final volume of 20 mL per vial (CroFab is dosed in the number of vials, not an SI-based unit of measure).
    - The total volume to add to be further diluted is
      - x mL / 4 vials = 20 mL / 1 vial
      - solving for x mL = 20 mL x 4 vials / 1 vial
      - x mL = 80 mL
    - To correctly dilute this volume of 80 mL to a final total of 250 mL of normal saline, we must first withdraw the volume from the normal saline.
      - In normal saline IV bags, there is 25 mL of overfill in the 250 mL product.
        - (275 mL + 80 mL) - x mL = 250 mL
        - Solving for x mL = (275 mL + 80 mL) - 250 mL = x mL
        - x mL = 105 mL.
          - Therefore, before adding the drug, we must FIRST remove 105 mL and then add 80 mL of CroFab.
      - The 250 mL total volume is administered over 1 hour with the final product appropriately labeled.
      - We must now determine the IV infusion rate in mL per minute to program the IV pump.
      - 250 mL / 1 hour x 1 hour / 60 minutes = 4.2 mL/minute

IV Drip Rates by Drop

- **When no IV pump is available, infusion rates are calculated using IV drip counters.**

    - Between 10 to 60 drops equal 1 mL.
    - An infusion rate in mL/minute can be determined by counting the number of drops per minute.

- **A provider in an acute care hospital receives a call from an EMS paramedic, transferring a critically ill patient to your facility.**

    - They need assistance determining the appropriate infusion rate for an epinephrine drip compounded using 1 mg of epinephrine in 1000 mL of normal saline.
    - Agreeing that the desired dose is 5 mcg/minute, how many drops per minute should the paramedic observe using a 20 gtt/mL infusion set?
        - 1 mg / 1000mL x 1000 mcg / 1 mg = 1000 mcg / 1000 mL
        - The final concentration = 1 mcg / 1 mL
        - The desired dose by volume at 5 mcg/minute is x mL / 5 mcg = 1 mL / 1 mcg
        - x = 5 mL, or 5 mL/minute
        - Finally, determining the number of drops per minute:
            - x drops / 5 mL = 20 drops / 1 mL
            - x drops = 20 drops x 5 mL / 1 mL
            - x = 100 drops per minute
                - Therefore, you instruct the paramedic to adjust the drip rate to count 100 drops per minute.

High-Yield Med Reviews

MPJE
Review Course

TEXAS
State Specific Laws & Regulations

This Rapid Review is based on the NABP MPJE Competency Statements which summarize the topics covered on the exam. The Competency Statements provide an *outline* to aid in preparation for the exam, however this review also includes additional key elements in the laws that are essential to know when preparing for the state MPJE.

- The NABP MPJE Competency Statements do NOT include all exam content.
- No distinction is made between federal and state jurisprudence questions on the MPJE. You must answer each question based on the state's prevailing laws where you seek licensure.
- The best preparation for the MPJE combines formal education, training, practical experience, and self-study.
- Additional information may also be obtained from the licensing state board of pharmacy.

If you have not done so yet, we recommend you watch our short video on how to study for the MPJE using our program.

SCAN ME

STATE BOARD OF PHARMACY (BOP) STRUCTURE

- **BOP Members**
  (Texas Pharmacy Act § 551-553)

  - Consists of 11 Governor-appointed members with subsequent consent of the State Senate.
  - Serve staggered 6-year terms (3-4 members' terms expire every other year).
    - Maximum of 2 consecutive, full terms
  - 7 Pharmacist BOP Members
    - Member pharmacists must be employed in Class A and Class C Pharmacies.
    - Must be practicing and residing in Texas.
    - Licensed for 5 years before BOP appointment.
  - 3 Non-pharmacist BOP Members
    - Cannot be certified, licensed, or registered with a regulatory agency in healthcare.
    - Cannot own more than 10% interest in a business regulated by the BOP.
  - 1 PT BOP Member
    - Must be practicing and residing in Texas.
    - Registered for 5 years before BOP appointment.
  - Oversee the Texas Prescription Monitoring Program (PMP).

> **Fast Facts**
>
> ✓ *Not all members of the BOP are pharmacists! Members include 3 members who are not pharmacists (healthcare professionals at all), and 1 member who is a PT.*

- **BOP Meetings**
  - BOP meetings are held quarterly to discuss and formulate public policy with regard to pharmacy practice and act in accordance with the Texas Open Meetings Act.
  - BOP members receive input from members of the public through task forces, public hearings, public forums, electronic media, and other forms of communication.

LICENSURE AND PERSONNEL

- **Pharmacists**
  (Texas Pharmacy Act § 558-562; Texas Pharmacy Rules § 283)

  - New Applicants
    - ≥ 18 years old and of good moral character
    - 1,500 hours from a BOP-approved internship
    - Professional practice degree from an accredited pharmacy degree program
    - Passed the NAPLEX and MPJE.
    - No license restrictions, suspensions, revocations, or surrender for any reason.
    - Initial license fee is $338.
    - License is valid for 2 years.

  - Transfer or Reciprocity
    - License must have never been suspended, revoked, canceled, surrendered, or otherwise restricted.
    - Transferring states must grant reciprocal licenses to pharmacists licensed in Texas.
    - Must take and pass the MPJE.
    - Pay the reciprocity fee of $255.
    - License is valid for 2 years.

  - Foreign Graduate
    - Pharmacy degree conferred by a school that is not ACPE-accredited but listed in the World Directory of Schools of Pharmacy (by the World Health Organization).
    - Obtain full certification from the Foreign Pharmacy Graduate Equivalency Committee (FPGEC) through the National Association of Boards of Pharmacy (NABP).
      - May reciprocate from any valid state license after full FPGEC certification.
    - Can qualify for an extended internship if they apply to take the NAPLEX and MPJE within 6 months after obtaining FPGEC certification.
      - BOP-approved internships include 6 months from the beginning of FPGEC certification and expire 6 months later if the NAPLEX and MPJE are not passed.
      - An extended internship remains in effect for 2 years but expires with the following:
        - Passing the NAPLEX and MPJE within a 6-month window and obtaining a license.
        - Failure of the NAPLEX and/or MPJE.
        - Failure to take the NAPLEX and MPJE within 6 months of graduation or FPGEC certification.
        - Residency termination.
      - Hours can be acquired in states other than Texas if they have been approved and certified to Texas by another state BOP.
    - Minimum number of 1740 hours of internship is required.

  - Continuing Education (CE)
    - Minimum of 30 hours of CE credits
    - Live programs, home study, or other mediated instruction
    - 1 hour on Texas pharmacy law or rules biennially
    - 3 hours of preceptor training biennially (for preceptor recertification)
    - Non-traditional CE credit

- Passing the NAPLEX = 30 hours, counting as an exemption for the first licensure cycle
- Advanced Cardiac Life Support (ACLS) initial certification = 12 hours
- Public board meeting = 3 hours
- Passing certain certification examinations (i.e., BPS) = 3 hours

— Cannot duplicate a license or license renewal certificate to practice pharmacy.
  — Pocket license cards can be photocopied.

- **Pharmacy Interns (PI)**
  (Texas Pharmacy Act § 557; Texas Pharmacy Rules § 283.4-283.6, 295)

  — Registered with the BOP and enrolled in their first year at a Texas Pharmacy School.
  — Completed the first professional year of pharmacy school with at least 30 professional degree credit hours.
  — Completed BOP application.
  — Cleared relevant background checks.
  — Extended internship eligibility or special situations
    — Passed NAPLEX and MPJE but did not have sufficient internship hours.
    — Graduated pharmacy school within the prior 3 months but has only *applied* to take the NAPLEX and MPJE.
    — Texas pharmacist license expired (2-10 years ago, has passed the MPJE, but lacks a sufficient number of internship hours.
    — Ordered by the BOP to complete an internship.
  — Under the supervision of a pharmacist
    — Completed the technician training program for that pharmacy.
    — Completed sterile training, if applicable.
    — Cannot identify themselves, sign, or initial any document, or independently supervise technicians as a pharmacist.
  — Not under the supervision of a pharmacist
    — PI functions as a PT but does not have to register as a PT if they have been registered with the BOP.
  — PIs are NOT counted in the ratio of pharmacists:PTs.
  — Pharmacist preceptor requirements
    — Active pharmacist license with no BOP imposed penalty within the previous 3 years
    — At least 1 year of experience or 6 months of residency (ASHP-accredited).
    — Complete 3 hours of pharmacist preceptor training (ACPE-approved provider, SOP) within the previous two years and with biennial renewal to continue the certification.
    — May be applied toward license renewal.

- **Pharmacy Technicians (PT)**
  (Texas Pharmacy Act § 568; Texas Pharmacy Rules § 297)

  — Registered PT
    — Successfully passed the National PT Certification exam (or equivalent), completed the registration application, and paid the required fee.
    — Complete 20 hours of CE every licensing period (including 1 hour of pharmacy law) with records maintained for 3 years from the reporting date.

 Fast Facts

✓ *Like pharmacists, PTs are required to complete CE every licensing period. Instead of 30 hours like pharmacists, PTs are required to obtain 20 hours each licensing period.*

- Performs nonjudgmental technical duties for the preparation and distribution of prescription drugs.
- Core functions
  - Refill authorization requests (but not refill authorizations from the prescriber)
  - Starting electronic transfer requests with pharmacies sharing an electronic prescription database
  - Entering prescription data into a data processing system
  - Preparing and packaging drug orders from bulk stock
  - Adding prescription labels (and other labels) to prescription bottles
  - Reconstituting, prepackaging, and labeling prepackaged drugs
  - Loading bulk, unlabeled drugs into an automated dispensing system
    - A pharmacist must verify after loading before use.
  - Nonsterile and sterile compounding
- PT Trainee
  - Applied to the BOP and underwent a training process to become a PT.
  - Registrations expire after 2 years (non-renewable).
- Certificates (PT or PT trainee) must be publicly displayed at the primary place of employment.

- **Pharmacist to PT ratio – 1:4** (exceptions below)

  - One PT must be a registered PT (not a PT trainee).
  - 1:5 if the pharmacy dispenses no more than 20 different drugs and no sterile products
  - There is no specified pharmacist-in-training (PIT) to pharmacist ratio.

- **Discipline**
  (Texas Pharmacy Rules §281.7)

  - The BOP may discipline an applicant or the holder of a current or expired license when they:
    - Violated a BOP rule.
    - Engaged in unprofessional conduct.
    - Engaged in gross immorality.
    - Demonstrated incompetency in their practice of pharmacy with reasonable skill.
    - Engaged in pharmacy practice fraud, deceit, or misrepresentation, including while seeking a license to practice pharmacy.
    - Convicted of or placed on deferred adjudication of a misdemeanor.
    - Convicted of a felony.
    - Used alcohol or drugs in an intemperate manner that, according to the BOP, could endanger a patient's life.
    - Aided or abetted an unlicensed person in the practice of pharmacy.
    - Disciplined by the regulatory Board of another state for substantially equivalent conduct in that state.
  - Disciplinary Actions by the BOP may include administrative penalties, suspension, revocation, or restriction of a person's license, refusal to issue or renew the person's license, placement of the offender's license on probation and under supervision, reprimanding the person, retiring the person's license, or imposing more than one sanction.

PHARMACY CLASSIFICATION

- **Structure and Organization**
  (Texas Pharmacy Rules § 291.33)

    - Pharmacy must be organized, clean, lighted, and ventilated.
    - Equipment must be in good operating condition.
    - Sink with hot and cold running water should be within the pharmacy (not in the restroom).
    - Temperature must be maintained within a range appropriate for storing prescription drugs in the refrigerator and the pharmacy.
    - Class A pharmacies must have an area suitable for confidential patient counseling.
        - Must be easily accessible to both patients and pharmacists.
        - Patients must not have access to prescription drugs.
        - Maintains confidentiality and privacy of patient communication.
    - No animals (other than fish in aquariums) are permitted within the pharmacy or adjacent areas.

- **Equipment**
  (Texas Pharmacy Rules § 291.33)

    - Data processing system, including a printer or comparable equipment
    - Refrigerator
    - Adequate supply of child-resistant, light-resistant, tight, and, if applicable, glass containers
    - Adequate supply of prescription, poison, and other applicable labels
    - Appropriate equipment necessary for the proper preparation of prescription drug orders
    - Metric-apothecary weight and measure conversion charts

- **Records**
  (Texas Pharmacy Rules § 291.33)

    - Inventory records must be kept by the pharmacy at the pharmacy's licensed location and be available for at least 2 years from the date of the inventory.
        - Must be accessible within 72 hours if requested by the BOP.
        - For eScripts (electronic format), requested records must be provided in a mutually agreeable format.

- **References**
  (Texas Pharmacy Rules § 291.33)

    - Pharmacy must maintain a library with current hard copies or electronic versions of specific information.
    - Class A Pharmacies (Community Pharmacy)
        - Texas Pharmacy Act and Rules, Texas Dangerous Drug Act, Texas CS Act and Rules, and the Federal CS Act.
        - United States Pharmacopeia (USP) Dispensing Information, Volume II (advice to the patient) or a reference text or leaflets that provide patient information.
        - Drug interactions reference
        - One of the following:
            - AHFS, Clinical Pharmacology, Facts & Comparisons, USP Volume I, Remington's Pharmaceutical Sciences

— Basic antidote information and telephone number to the nearest Poison Control Center (1-800-222-1222)

- **Security**
  (Texas Pharmacy Rules § 291.33)

  — When the pharmacist is not actively on-site, the prescription department must be locked (by key, combination, or another mechanical or electrical lock) to stop unauthorized access.
    — Never duplicate the lock key or code without the authorization of the PIC or the owner.

- **Class A Pharmacy – Community Pharmacy**
  (Texas Pharmacy Rules§ 291.31-291.36)

  — Personnel Roles
    — One full-time PIC per Class A pharmacy is designated.
      — May only be a PIC at Class A pharmacies open simultaneously.
      — PIC of a Class A pharmacy cannot be a PIC of a Class B or Class C pharmacy with ≥ 101 beds.
    — PIC responsibilities
      — Educating and training PTs, supervising appropriate procurement of any products dispensed, disposing of and distributing drugs, storing all drugs, chemicals, and biologicals, maintaining all necessary records/documents, and legally operating the pharmacy.
    — Owners of a Class A pharmacy shall have responsibility for all administrative and operational functions of the pharmacy.
    — Pharmacists in Class A
      — Receiving oral prescription drug orders for CS and reducing these orders to writing, either manually or electronically
      — Interpreting prescription drug orders and selecting drug products
      — Performing the final check of the dispensed prescription before delivery to the patient
      — Interpreting patient medication records and performing drug regimen reviews

⚖️ **Law Pearl**

✓ *This is a concept to consider the scenario of a PT-check-PT program. In a Class A pharmacy that uses an AMS, PTs may be the professionals who load the AMS, and when dispensed for a patient prescription, checked by a PT. HOWEVER, this still requires a final check by the pharmacist on duty. The PT-check-PT functions include filling medication carts, floor stock supplies, and accessing and restocking AMSs.*

      — Performing a specific act of drug therapy management for a patient delegated to a pharmacist by a written protocol from a physician licensed in Texas that complies with the Medical Practice Act
      — Responsible for the legal operation of the pharmacy.
      — Solely responsible for the direct supervision of PTs and PT trainees.
        — Electronic supervision of PTs by the pharmacist can be done when the PT is entering prescription data into the data processing system.
        — Pharmacists can supervise PTs from another facility provided that the pharmacist is employed by a Class E pharmacy that has the same owner as the Class A pharmacy where the PTs are located or has entered into a written contract or agreement with the Class A pharmacy, which outlines the provided

services, responsibilities, and accountabilities.

- **Class B Pharmacy – Nuclear Pharmacy**
  (Texas Pharmacy Rules § 291.51-291.55)

  - Structure and Operations
    - If Class A functions are also performed, and the pharmacy is already licensed as Class B, no additional license requirement is needed, but it must follow all Class A and B laws and regulations.
    - Radioactive drug service describes the process of distributing radiopharmaceuticals, participation in radiopharmaceutical selection, and performance of radiopharmaceutical drug reviews.
    - Radiopharmaceuticals are prescription drugs or devices that exhibit spontaneous disintegration of unstable nuclei with the emission of a nuclear particle(s) or photon(s), including any nonradioactive reagent kit or radionuclide generator that is intended to be used in the preparation of any such substance.
    - Required to be equipped with the necessary equipment to provide radioactive drug services.
      - Key examples include a dose calibrator, vertical laminar flow hood, microscope, hemocytometer, scintillation analyzer, and radiation monitoring devices.
    - An authorized nuclear pharmacist may only distribute radiopharmaceuticals to authorized users for patient use.
    - All radiopharmaceutical drugs must be stored at the proper temperature, as defined in the USP-NF.
    - The pharmacy's generator must be stored and eluted in an ISO Class 7 or 8 environment.
    - Labels
      - In addition to standard label requirements, the outer container must also contain "caution-radioactive material" or "danger, radioactive material," the amount of radioactive material contained in millicuries (mCi), microcuries (uCi), or becquerels (Bq), and the corresponding time that applies to this activity, if different from the requested calibration date and time.
    - Nuclear pharmacy equipment requirements include a vertical laminar flow hood, dose calibrator, a calibrated system or device to monitor temperature, Class A prescription balance, analytical balance and weights, scintillation analyzer, microscope, hemocytometer, and equipment and utensils necessary for the proper compounding of a prescription drug or medication orders.
  - Personnel Roles
    - PIC
      - Employed full-time and PIC for only one Class B and no Class A or C pharmacy with $\geq$ 101 beds.
        - May be PIC at more than one Class B pharmacy if the other Class B pharmacies are not providing pharmacy services simultaneously.
        - During an emergency, a PIC may oversee up to two Class B pharmacies that are open simultaneously if the PIC works $\geq$ 10 hours per week in each pharmacy for no more than a period of 30 consecutive days.
      - Must ensure that all pharmacy personnel responsible for compounding and/or supervising the compounding of radiopharmaceuticals within the pharmacy receive appropriate education, training, and competency evaluations.
    - Authorized nuclear pharmacists
      - General qualifications

- Completion of Texas Regulations for Control of Radiation of the Radiation Control Program, Texas Department of State Health Services
- Board certified in nuclear pharmacy by the Board of Pharmaceutical Specialties or having a written certification of achievement of a level of competency sufficient to operate as an authorized nuclear pharmacist independently with satisfactory completion of 700 hours in a structured educational program.
  - All personnel performing tasks in the preparation and distribution of radiopharmaceuticals shall be under the direct supervision of an authorized nuclear pharmacist.
- The ratio of authorized nuclear pharmacists to PTs or PT trainees is 1:3.
  - May change to 1:6 if at least 3 of the 6 PTs are trained in handling radioactive materials.

- **Class C Pharmacy – Institutional Pharmacy**
  (Texas Pharmacy Rules § 291.71-291.77)

  - Structure and Operations
    - Class C pharmacies include hospitals, other patient facilities, hospice patient facilities, ambulatory surgical centers, or hospitals maintained or operated by the State of Texas.
    - Pharmacy must have received Class C-S pharmacy status for compounding sterile preparations.
    - Pharmacy must be enclosed and capable of being locked by key, combination, or other mechanical or electronic means.
      - Individuals authorized by the PIC (including nonpharmacy personnel) can enter the pharmacy.
    - Must have locked storage for CS II drugs and other drugs requiring additional security.
    - Some facilities may have the pharmacy close at specific times.
      - If so, when practitioners order a drug for administration, only sufficient quantities of drugs for immediate therapeutic needs can be removed from the institutional pharmacy by a designated licensed nurse or practitioner.
        - Must record the drug withdrawal.
      - When the pharmacist has returned, they must verify the drug withdrawals and perform a drug regimen review within 7 days.
    - These pharmacies cannot sell, purchase, trade, or possess prescription drug samples unless the pharmacy meets specific requirements.
    - Drugs may be prepackaged in quantities suitable for internal distribution by a pharmacist, PTs, or PT trainees under a pharmacist's direction and direct supervision.
      - Labels of prepackaged units shall indicate the brand or generic name, strength of the drug, manufacturer or distributor name, facility's unique lot number, expiration date based on the currently available literature, and quantity of the drug if the quantity is greater than one.
        - Records of prepackaging must include the name of the drug, strength, dosage form, facility's unique lot number, manufacturer or distributor, manufacturer's lot number, expiration date, quantity per prepackaged unit, number of prepackaged units, date packaged, name, initials, or electronic signature of the

> **⌒ Accelerate Your Knowledge**
>
> ✓ *Most consider that all Class C pharmacies require C-S certification, however, this is not the case. Specific ambulatory surgical centers that range from orthopedics to dental surgery centers utilize a wide variety of drugs for analgesia, sedation, antibiotics, and others, but do not necessarily seek C-S certification. From their utilization of third-party compounding pharmacies, and nursing or anesthesia administered medication, the need for sterile compounding capacity is unnecessary.*

person packaging, and name, initials, or electronic signature of the responsible pharmacist.

- If sterile preparations are prepared in a location other than the pharmacy, a specific supplementary label must be affixed to the container of any admixture.
- Drugs may be given to patients in facilities only on the order of a practitioner.
  - No change in a drug or order may be made without the approval of a practitioner except as authorized by the practitioner.
  - PTs and PT trainees may not receive oral medication orders.
- Facility with ≤ 100 beds
  - Must have a pharmacist at least on a part-time or consulting basis and at least once every 7 days.
    - Must be accessible at all times to respond to all questions and needs.
  - One employed or contracted PIC may be PIC for ≤ 3 facilities or 150 beds.
    - Alternatively, can be PIC at one facility with ≥ 101 beds and one facility with ≤ 100 beds, including a rural hospital, as long as the total number of beds is ≤ 150 beds.

> ⚖️ **Law Pearl**
>
> ✓ This might seem confusing to professionals in major cities, but in the large rural area of Texas, these hospitals are widely present. Since the low population areas they serve naturally have a low population of pharmacists, this limited staffing necessity is reasonable. Additionally, as technology advances, these are being more widely managed by third-party, off-site pharmacists who are electronically present 24/7, with minimum physical presence exercised.

- Facility with ≥ 101 beds
  - A pharmacy must have continuous on-site supervision when it is open for pharmacy services.
    - Without physical supervision by a pharmacist, PTs or PT trainees may distribute prepackaged and prelabeled drugs from a drug storage area of the facility (i.e., a surgery suite) if a pharmacist controls the distribution.
  - Full-time PIC can only be at one location, including Class A or B pharmacies.
- Rural Hospitals
  - Defined as a licensed hospital with ≤ 75 beds located in a county with a population of ≤ 50,000 or has been designated by the Centers for Medicare and Medicaid Services as a critical access hospital, rural referral center, or sole community hospital.
  - PTs at these locations must be trained on the procedures for accuracy verification of actions performed by PTs, including duties that may and may not be performed by PTs in the absence of a pharmacist and the PT's role in preventing dispensing and distribution errors.
- Automated Devices and Systems
  - Automated compounding or counting devices (ACD)
    - Must have a protocol for calibration and verification of compounding accuracy.
    - Must document the calibration and verification on a routine basis.
  - May contain unlabeled drugs, with the ACD producing a label upon dispensing.
    - Unlabeled drug records must include the name of the drug, strength, dosage form, manufacturer or distributor, lot number, expiration date, loading date, name, initials, or electronic signature of the person loading the ACD, and signature or electronic signature of the responsible pharmacist.
    - ACD shall not be used until a pharmacist verifies that the system is properly loaded.

- Automated Medication Supply Systems (AMS)
  (Texas Administrative Code § 291)
  - AMS must be available for inspection by the BOP to validate its accuracy.
  - Quality assurance programs must maintain continuous monitoring of the AMS system.

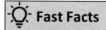

Fast Facts

✓ AMS systems may sound similar to ACDs, but consider common names, such as Pyxis, Omnicell, or MediTech, to make types of AMS systems more recognizable.

  - Should be programmed for a pharmacist's review and approval of each original or new medication order before withdrawal from the AMS, except for an emergency order.
    - Can be done within 72 hours when a full-time pharmacist is not on duty when the order is made, or retrospectively within 7 days in a facility with a part-time or consultant pharmacist when a pharmacist is not on duty when the order is made.
  - AMS systems can store and record medication use outside the pharmacy department (i.e., Pyxis).
    - A PT or PT trainee can restock an AMS outside the pharmacy when a pharmacist verifies that the drugs pulled to stock the AMS system match the list of prescription drugs generated by the AMS system.
  - AMS system documents and maintains:
    - Name(s), initials, or identification code(s) of each pharmacist responsible for the check.
    - Name(s), initials, or identification code(s) and specific activities of each pharmacist, PT, or PT trainee who performs any other portion of the medication order preparation process.
- Automated Checking Device
  - ACDs are fully automated devices that confirm the correct drug and strength have been labeled with the correct label for the correct patient after a drug is prepared for distribution but before delivery to the patient.
  - Can perform the final check of a drug prepared if a pharmacist conducts the check of the final product before delivery to the patient or a pharmacist performs certain checks (prepackaged drug used to fill the order is verified by a pharmacist, and new prescription drug orders are verified for accuracy).
- Personnel Roles
  - PIC shall ensure that drug utilization reviews and drug regimen reviews are conducted.
    - PIC must collaborate with other healthcare practitioners to ensure that patients or their caregivers receive information regarding drugs and their safe and effective use.
  - Pharmacists on duty can dispense drugs to outpatients, including patients in an emergency department and outpatient radiology (i.e., X-ray, CT scan, or MRI).
    - If there is no pharmacist on duty in the facility, the following is applicable for supplying prescription drugs:
      - Only specific prescription medications and CS that are listed on the emergency room drug list may be supplied.
        - Developed by the PIC and emergency department committee consisting of drugs to meet the immediate needs of emergency room patients.
      - Dispensed with ≤ 72-hour supply in suitable containers that are appropriately prelabeled by the institutional pharmacy.
    - PIC or delegate must verify the dispensing record at least once every 7 days.
  - Pharmacists
    - Assist the PIC in meeting their responsibilities.

- Ensure the drug is prepared for distribution safely and accurately as prescribed.
  - Pharmacy's data processing system may record the identity of each pharmacist involved in a specific portion of the preparation of medication.
- A pharmacist must receive, interpret, and evaluate medication orders (not prescriptions).
- Pharmacists may also participate in drug or device selection, drug administration, drug regimen review, or drug or drug-related research.
  - A written protocol from a licensed physician must be created.
- PT
  - In Class C pharmacies or other facilities with clinical pharmacy programs, PT-check-PT may be used if PTs have been properly trained.
  - PT-check-PT functions may include filling medication carts or floor stock supplies and accessing and restocking automated medication supply systems.
  - Facility with ≥ 101 beds
    - May pre-pack and label unit- and multiple-dose packages provided a pharmacist supervises, conducts a final check, and affixes their name, initials, or electronic signature to the appropriate quality control records before distribution.
    - May prepare, package, compound, or label prescription drugs according to medication orders, providing a pharmacist supervises and checks the preparation before distribution.
- A pharmacist must be physically present to directly supervise PT or PT trainees.
  - Electronic supervision may be done in a facility with ≤ 100 beds.
- No pharmacist-to-PT ratio limitations

- **Class D Pharmacy – Clinic Pharmacy**
(Texas Pharmacy Rules § 291.91-291.94)

  - Structure and Operations
    - A clinic is a facility or location except for a physician's office with various dangerous drugs and devices on its formulary, and the drugs may be stored, administered, provided, or dispensed to outpatients.
    - A pharmacy operated by the state or a local government that qualifies for a Class D license is not required to pay a fee to obtain a license
    - Facility has no more than 6 temporary and simultaneously operating locations.
      - Must notify the BOP of the locations of the temporary locations where drugs will be provided and the schedule for the operation of such clinics.
      - Must notify the BOP within 10 days of a change in address, closing of a temporary location, or a change in the schedule of operation of a clinic.
    - Must have a formulary that lists all drugs and devices administered, dispensed, or provided by the Class D pharmacy.
      - Formulary components include anti-infectives, musculoskeletal drugs, vitamins, obstetric and gynecologic drugs, topical drugs, vitamins, serums, toxoids, and vaccines.
      - No CSs may be stored at a Class D pharmacy.
      - May not contain injectable drugs for administration in the clinic or nonprescription drugs.
        - Also, cannot contain nalbuphine, drugs to treat erectile dysfunction, & CS I–V
      - If the patient population served is at least 80% indigent, the PIC may petition the BOP to operate with a formulary that includes types of drugs and devices other than those listed above or that are normally excluded.

- Drugs and/or devices may only be provided in prepackaged quantities in suitable and/or original manufacturer's containers that are appropriately labeled.
- No dangerous drugs can be stored or left for later pickup by the patient at the temporary location(s), and all drugs are returned to the permanent location each day in the pharmacy or its mobile unit that is secured from unauthorized access.
- The clinic pharmacy has a Pharmacy and Therapeutics Committee composed of at least 3 persons: the PIC, the clinic's medical director, and a person responsible for providing drugs and devices.
    - Personnel Roles
        - One PIC must be employed at least part-time under a written agreement.
            - May supervise an unlimited number of Class D pharmacies.
            - Provide continuous supervision of registered nurses, licensed vocational nurses, PAs, PTs or PT trainees, and assistants carrying out the pharmacy-related aspects of care.
            - Responsible for formulary development with the clinic's Pharmacy and Therapeutics Committee
        - PIC, consultant pharmacist, or staff pharmacist will personally visit the clinic on at least a monthly basis to ensure that the clinic is following established policies and procedures.
            - Clinics operated by state or local governments and clinics funded by government sources of money may petition the BOP for an alternative visitation schedule.
        - Staff pharmacists and the consultant pharmacist (who may be PIC) shall assist the PIC or any delegated act performed by supportive personnel under their supervision.
        - Staff pharmacists and consultant pharmacists are responsible for any delegated act performed by supportive personnel under their supervision.
            - Supportive personnel (not necessarily PT or PT trainees) shall be qualified to perform the pharmacy tasks assigned to them.
        - Pharmacy owner is responsible for all administrative and operational functions of the pharmacy that the PIC may guide.

- **Class E Pharmacy – Nonresident (Out-of-State) Pharmacy**
(Texas Pharmacy Rules § 291.101-291.106)
    - Structure and Operations
        - Class E pharmacies are located outside of Texas and dispense prescription drugs or devices under a prescription drug order and deliver the drug or device to a patient in Texas by mail, a common carrier, or a delivery service. May also process prescription orders for patients or perform other pharmaceutical sources defined by the BOP.
        - A Class E pharmacy shall be under the continuous on-site supervision of a pharmacist licensed in the state in which the Class E pharmacy is located.
        - Must have a licensed pharmacist in Texas to serve as the PIC of the Class E pharmacy license.
        - Class E pharmacy personnel cannot compound sterile preparations unless the pharmacy has applied for and obtained a Class E-S pharmacy.
            - Must comply with regulations like a C-S pharmacy.
        - If prescriptions are routinely delivered outside the area covered by the pharmacy's local telephone service, the pharmacy shall provide a toll-free telephone line that is answered during normal business hours to enable communication between the patient and a pharmacist.

⚖ **Law Pearl**

✓ *Consider specific clinical scenarios. For example, a patient who lives in Texas receives a rare medication for outpatient chemotherapy. This medication is available at only a few pharmacies in the US, so the drug may have to be obtained through a mail-order pharmacy. In this case, the mail-order pharmacy must abide by the regulations of Texas Class E Pharmacies.*

- Unless compliance would violate the pharmacy or drug laws or rules in the state in which the pharmacy is located, a pharmacist in a Class E pharmacy who dispenses a prescription for CS II – V for a resident of Texas shall electronically send the prescription information to the Texas State Board of Pharmacy.
- Personnel Roles
    - A pharmacist can use professional judgment not to dispense a prescription drug if the pharmacist knows that the prescription was issued based on an internet-based or telephonic consultation without a valid patient-practitioner relationship.
    - Only a pharmacist may orally provide drug information to a patient or patient's agent and answer questions concerning prescription drugs.
        - Non-pharmacist personnel may not ask questions of a patient or patient's agent intended to screen and/or limit interaction with the pharmacist.
    - A pharmacist in a Class E pharmacy may not refuse to transfer prescriptions to another pharmacy on behalf of the patient.
        - Must be done within 4 business days of the request.

- **Class F Pharmacy – Emergency Medical Care Center Pharmacy**
(Texas Pharmacy Rules § 291.151)

    - **Structure and Operations**
        - A freestanding emergency medical care facility (FEMCF) is a facility that is licensed by the Texas Department of State Health Services to provide emergency care to patients.
        - Pharmacies in FEMCFs are areas in the facilities, separate from patient care areas, where drugs are stored, bulk compounded, delivered, compounded, dispensed, and/or distributed to other areas or departments of the FEMCF or dispensed to an ultimate user or their agent.
        - Each FEMCF should have a designated pharmacy work area separate from patient areas, have space adequate for the size and scope of pharmaceutical services, and have adequate space and security for the storage of drugs.
        - May stock CS drugs in locked storage.
        - Pharmacy and storage areas for prescription drugs and/or devices shall be enclosed and capable of being locked by key, combination, or other mechanical or electronic means to prohibit access by unauthorized individuals. Only individuals authorized by the PIC may enter the pharmacy or access storage areas for prescription drugs and/or devices.
        - Drugs may be administered to patients in FEMCFs only on the order of a practitioner.
            - Pharmacists may be granted approval to interchange drugs based on the facility's formulary, which is approved by the medical staff of the FEMCF.
                - Practitioners may override the interchange.
            - No changes may be made without the approval of a practitioner.

Fast Facts

✓ The "doc in the box" emergency medical care facilities are not operationally like emergency departments in healthcare institutions. The main consideration here is that there is no pharmacist onsite, with a single pharmacist acting as PIC who may only be a part-time employee.

        - In facilities using a floor stock method of drug distribution, the pharmacy shall establish designated floor stock areas outside the central pharmacy where drugs may be stored.
    - Personnel Roles
        - Must have 1 PIC employed or under contract, at least on a consulting or part-time basis, but may be employed full-time.

- **Class G Pharmacy – Central Prescription Drug or Medication Order Processing Pharmacy**
  (Texas Pharmacy Rules § 291.153)

  - Structure and Operations
    - A facility established for the primary purpose of processing prescription drugs or medication drug orders.
      - Class A, Class C, or Class E Pharmacies may outsource prescription drug or medication order processing to a Class G pharmacy, provided the pharmacies have the same owner or have entered into a written contract or agreement.
        - Outlines the services to be provided and the responsibilities and accountabilities of each pharmacy.
        - Share a common electronic file or have the appropriate technology to allow access to sufficient information necessary or required to perform a non-dispensing function.
    - Therefore, it must comply with Class A, C, and E regulations.
    - Process prescription drug or medication orders on behalf of another pharmacy, healthcare provider, or payor.

> ⚖️ **Law Pearl**
>
> ✓ *A Class G pharmacy that provides services to Class A, C, or E pharmacies must comply with all the laws pertaining to those classes, in addition to Class G pharmacy laws.*

    - This does not include dispensing a prescription drug but includes receiving, interpreting, or clarifying prescription drug or medication orders, entering data, transferring prescription drug or medication order information, performing drug regimen reviews, obtaining refill and substitution authorizations, verifying accurate prescription data entry, interpreting clinical data for prior authorization for dispensing, performing therapeutic interventions, and providing drug information concerning a patient's prescription.
  - Personnel Roles
    - PIC
      - Must have 1 PIC employed full-time at only 1 Class G pharmacy.
    - Pharmacists shall directly supervise PT and PT trainees who enter prescription data into the pharmacy's data processing system by one of the following methods:
      - Electronic supervision if they are able to communicate directly with the PT or PT trainee immediately and have immediate access to any original document containing prescription or medication order information or other information related to the dispensing of the prescription or medication order.
        - Verifies the accuracy of the data entered before the release of information to the system for storage.
      - Direct supervision
    - Pharmacists will verify data entry of the prescription drug or medication order information at the time of data entry before the release of the information to Class A, C, or E pharmacies for dispensing.
    - Identification of pharmacy personnel
      - All pharmacists, pharmacist interns, PTs, and PT trainees must wear an identification tag or badge that bears the person's name and identifies them as a PT or a certified PT.

GENERAL PHARMACY FUNCTIONS

- **Prescription Labels**
  (Texas Pharmacy Act § 562)

  - Medication brand name
    - If there is no brand name, then list the generic name, the drug's strength, and the drug's manufacturer or distributor.
  - Specific Class A and Class E pharmacy requirements
    - Patient name
      - For animals, the species and owner name
    - Prescription number and dispensing date
    - For generic drugs dispensed, the statement "SUBSTITUTED FOR BRAND NAME" or "SUBSTITUTED FOR" immediately preceding the brand name
    - Pharmacy name, address, and telephone number
    - Dispensing pharmacist name, initials, or ID code
    - Prescriber name
    - Directions for use and any necessary ancillary instructions
    - Quantity dispensed
    - Expiration date if dispensed in anything other than the original manufacturer's container
    - "Do not flush unused medications or pour down the sink or drain" when applicable.
  - Prescriptions filled from a handwritten prescription
    - Diagnosis must be present.
    - Quantity must be a number and a word [i.e., #30 (thirty)].

- **Generic Substitution**
  (Texas Pharmacy Rules § 309)

  - Generically equivalent means that a drug is pharmaceutically and therapeutically equivalent to the drug prescribed.
  - Generic products are generally less expensive.
  - Patient must accept a generic substitution.
  - If the brand name drug must be dispensed, "DAW," "Brand Necessary," or "Brand Medically Necessary" should be handwritten on the prescription.
    - Can be stated on a verbal prescription.
    - Two-line prescription forms, check boxes, or other notifications on an original prescription do not prohibit a pharmacist from generic substitution.
  - For substituted products, the patient must be notified directly (or through an agent) before dispensing and provided the opportunity to choose the brand over a generic.
  - A clearly visible sign must appear in public view in at least 1-inch block letters in both English and Spanish, stating the following: "TEXAS LAW REQUIRES A PHARMACIST TO INFORM YOU IF A LESS EXPENSIVE GENERICALLY EQUIVALENT DRUG IS AVAILABLE FOR CERTAIN BRAND NAME DRUGS AND TO ASK YOU TO CHOOSE BETWEEN THE GENERIC AND THE BRAND NAME DRUG. YOU HAVE A RIGHT TO ACCEPT OR REFUSE THE GENERICALLY EQUIVALENT DRUG."
  - Drug or product terminology
    - Biological product
      - Wide-ranging definitions include a virus, therapeutic serum, toxin, antitoxin, vaccine, blood, blood component or derivative, allergenic product, protein, or analogous product, or arsphenamine or derivative of arsphenamine (or any other trivalent organic

arsenic compound), applicable to the prevention, treatment, or cure of a disease or condition of human beings.
- Interchangeable medications
  - Related to biological products, this is a biological product designated as therapeutically equivalent to another product in the most recent edition or supplement of the FDA-approved Drug Products with Therapeutic Equivalence Evaluations, also known as the Orange Book.
- Pharmaceutically equivalent
  - These are drug products that have identical amounts of active chemical ingredients in the same dosage form that meet the identical compendia or other applicable standards of strength, quality, and purity according to the USP or another nationally recognized compendium.
  - Differs from a generic equivalent because inactive ingredients may be different.
- Therapeutically equivalent
  - These are pharmaceutically equivalent drug products that will provide the same efficacy with identical duration and intensity if given in the same amount.
- Generic equivalents must have pharmaceutical and therapeutic equivalency.

Dosage Form Substitution
(Texas Pharmacy Act § 562; Texas Pharmacy Rules § 309.3)

- Dosage forms can be dispensed differently from what is prescribed (i.e., tablets to capsules or liquid, or vice versa).
- Patient must consent to substitution.
- Pharmacist notifies the practitioner of the substitution and what was dispensed.
- Limitations
  - No change in the amount of the active drug.
  - If an immediate release dosage form, the substitution cannot be a delayed/time release/enteric-coated product.
  - Must not affect desired clinical outcomes.
  - Cannot substitute for a compounded product.
  - Must receive authorization from the practitioner for the above (i.e., not a substitution).

> **Fast Facts**
>
> This is clinically valuable during drug shortages. An example would be amoxicillin SUSPENSION PO 400 mg BID being changed to amoxicillin CAPSULE/TABLET PO 400 mg BID if appropriate for the patient.

Patient Counseling
(Texas Pharmacy Rules § 291.33)

- Counseling consists of information deemed relevant by the pharmacist.
- Any new prescription or when requested by the patient or agent.
  - Not required for refill prescriptions, but it can be offered.
- It must be made orally and in person.
  - The counseling points must be reinforced with written information relevant to the prescription and provided to the patient or agent.
- Non-pharmacist personnel (ex., PTs) may not ask questions of a patient or patient's agent intended to screen or limit interaction with the pharmacist, or both.
- Counseling must be documented by recording the pharmacist's initials or identification code in the dispensing record.
- When the patient or agent refuses to counsel, the pharmacist must document the refusal.

- A sign (minimum 8.5" x 11") must be displayed in clear public view at all locations in the pharmacy where a patient may pick up prescriptions.
    - State in English and Spanish, "Do you have questions about your prescription? Ask the pharmacist." Such notification shall be in both English and Spanish.
- Delivered Prescriptions (ex., Amazon/PillPack)
    - Counseling should be delivered with the dispensed prescription in writing.
    - The following must be on the prescription container or a separate sheet delivered with the prescription container (in both English and Spanish)
        - The pharmacy's phone number
        - "Written information about this prescription has been provided for you. Please read this information before you take the medication. If you have questions concerning this prescription, a pharmacist is available during normal business hours to answer these questions at (insert the pharmacy's local and toll-free telephone numbers)."
    - The patient or agent must be informed that a pharmacist is available to discuss the prescription and provide information.

- **Prescription Records**
  (Texas Pharmacy Rules § 291.34)

    - Must be maintained and readily available by the pharmacy for 2 years from the date of initial dispensing.
        - For prescriptions with refills, records must be kept for 2 years from the last refill date.
    - Pharmacy inventory records must be kept for at least 2 years from the inventory date.
    - Records must be supplied within 72 hours in response to any BOP request.
    - Hard copy prescriptions must be stored using a 3-file method consisting of the following:
        - CS II files.
        - CS III - V files.
        - All non-CS files (including OTC).

- **Prescription Refills**
  (Texas Pharmacy Act § 562)

    - Accelerated refills include up to a 90-day supply of dangerous drugs under specific criteria.
        - Total quantity dispensed is not more than the total quantity of units permitted by the prescription, including all refills.
        - Patient consents to the dispensing of up to a 90-day supply.
            - Prescriber must be notified.
        - Prescriber does not indicate the medical necessity of initially dispensing only a certain quantity followed by refills.
        - Not permitted for psychotropic drugs.
        - Patient is $\geq$ 18 years of age.

- **Emergency Refills**
  (Texas Pharmacy Act § 562)

    - Does not include any CS II.
    - Under professional discretion, pharmacists may refill a prescription drug without the prescriber's authorization under specific circumstances.
        - Failing to refill the medication could disrupt a therapeutic regimen or create patient suffering.
        - Pharmacists cannot contact the prescriber after a reasonable effort, or a natural or artificial disaster prevents the pharmacist from contacting the prescriber.

- May dispense no more than a 72-hour supply.
- Patient must be notified at the time of dispensing by the pharmacist that the refill is being provided with no authorization, AND authorization from the prescriber must be provided for any refills.
- Pharmacists must notify the prescriber at the earliest reasonable time.
- Pharmacists must maintain a record of the emergency refill and relevant information.
- Pharmacist appropriately labels the prescription.
- For prescriptions initially filled at a different pharmacy, the pharmacist may utilize appropriate professional discretion to refill the prescription under specific circumstances.
    - Patient has the prescription container, receipt, label, or other documentation from the other pharmacy which contains the essential information.
    - Pharmacist is unable to contact the original pharmacy to transfer the remaining refills, or no refills are remaining.
    - An emergency refill is appropriate and follows all other requirements.
- Governor Declared Disaster - 30-Day Rule
    - Applies to natural and manufactured disasters (i.e., hurricanes or terrorist attacks, respectively) where the governor has declared a state of disaster, and the BOP has issued an executive order stating pharmacists may dispense up to a 30-day supply of drugs.
    - Pharmacists may dispense *a refill* (30-day supply) without the authorization of the prescriber provided:
        - It is NOT for a CS II drug.
        - Interruption of a therapeutic regimen or patient suffering may result from failure to refill the prescription.
        - Pharmacists are unable to contact the practitioner due to the natural disaster.

> **⏱ Accelerate Your Knowledge**
>
> ✓ *Many natural disasters have led to the need for emergency rules, including Hurricane Harvey in 2017. This is not limited to natural disasters. For example, the COVID-19 state of emergency manifested a mandatory lockdown and permitted authorization of a Governor Declared Disaster scenario for dispensing pharmacies that was compliant with this regulation.*

- **Transfers**
(Texas Pharmacy Rules § 291.34(g))

    - Non-CS prescriptions can be transferred without limitation up to the number of originally authorized refills.
        - Must be transferred orally or by fax from one pharmacist to another pharmacist.
            - Can be transferred by a pharmacy student intern, extended intern, or resident intern.
            - Electronic transfers CAN be initiated by a PT or PT trainee under the direct supervision of a pharmacist.
    - Original transferred prescription and the transferred prescription must be maintained for ≥ 2 years from the last refill date (NOT the original date written).
    - Transferring pharmacist
        - Write 'VOID' on the face of the original prescription or void in the data processing system.
        - On the reverse of the prescription, record:
            - Receiving pharmacy name and address.
            - DEA registration number of the receiving pharmacy (if a CS).
            - Name of the individual receiving the prescription drug order
            - Name of the individual transferring the prescription drug order
            - Transfer date
    - Receiving pharmacist
        - Write 'TRANSFER' on the face of the prescription or indicate transfer in the electronic system.

- Record the following in the data processing system:
    - Original prescription date.
    - Dispensing date.
    - Original prescription number.
    - Number of original refills.
    - Number of valid refills remaining.
    - Last refill date.
    - Transferring pharmacy name and address.
    - DEA registration number of the receiving pharmacy.
    - Pharmacist name transferring the prescription.
- Verbally confirm information received (read-back).

- **Prospective Drug Use Review**
(Texas Pharmacy Rules § 291.31; Texas Pharmacy Act § 562.110)

    - A review of the patient's drug therapy and prescription drug order or medication order prior to dispensing or distributing the drug.
    - Telepharmacy systems must provide for completing drug use reviews and patient counseling services by an electronic method.

- **Prescription Drug Returns**
(Texas Pharmacy Rules § 291.8)

    - Accepting a return of a prescription for resale or re-dispensing is illegal.
    - Exceptions:
        - Specific unused drugs may be returned to healthcare facilities regulated by the state if the medication is sealed in unopened, tamper-evident packaging and either individually packaged or packaged in unit-dose packaging.
            - This may include penal institutions and nursing homes, but hospital (inpatient) medications may also be returned to the pharmacy for re-dispensing.
        - FDA-approved unit-dose packaging of oral, parenteral, topical, or inhalant drugs
        - Multidose parenteral medications without doses being withdrawn

- **Prescription Drug Recalls**
(Texas Pharmacy Rules § 291.7)

    - PIC must create a written procedure for properly managing drug recalls by the manufacturer, including how to contact patients to whom the recalled drug products have been dispensed.
    - Remove recalled drugs from inventory within 24 hours after receipt of the recall notice and quarantine them until proper disposal or destruction occurs.

- **Drug Therapy Management Protocol**
(Texas Pharmacy Rules § 295.13; Texas Medical Practice Act § 157.101)

    - A formal practice relationship between a pharmacist and a physician.
    - Must outline care functions delegated to the pharmacist and the circumstances when the pharmacist can provide them (i.e., a protocol, standing orders, etc).
        - Delegation to a pharmacist for implementation, modification, or signing of drug orders must be subsequent to diagnosis, initial patient assessment, and a drug therapy order.
        - A copy of the protocol must be kept at least until the 7th anniversary of the protocol's expiration date.

- Can collaborate without a protocol, but the protocol delegates patient care functions to a pharmacist beyond the pharmacist's typical scope of practice.

- **Pharmacist Immunizations/Vaccinations**
(Texas Pharmacy Rules § 295.15)

  - For most vaccinations, patients must be $\geq$ 14 years old unless a physician refers their patient to a pharmacist as a result of a preexisting physician-patient relationship.
    - A pharmacist may administer influenza vaccinations to patients $\geq$ 7 years of age.
  - Immunizations and vaccinations may be administered by pharmacists when authorized via a written protocol from an authorized physician. The protocol must include the following:
    - Physician partner(s) in the protocol.
    - Specific pharmacist(s) authorized.
    - Location(s) where vaccine administration is permitted.
    - Specific immunizations and vaccinations the pharmacist is permitted to administer.
    - Activities that the pharmacist should follow in administering vaccines, including the procedures to follow in case of an adverse reaction and how the pharmacist can report the vaccinations to the physician.
    - Notification to the physician in the protocol within 24 hours of administering the immunization and primary care physician within 14 days of administration.
  - Pharmacists must have completed an Accreditation Council for Pharmaceutical Education (ACPE)-approved immunization course.
    - Specific content should include basic cardiac life support and hands-on training.
    - Must achieve a passing score in the course.
  - Minimum of 20 hours of instruction and experiential training required (with CDC training guidelines).

- **Pseudoephedrine Products**
(Texas Health and Safety Code Title 6(C) § 486)

  - Pseudoephedrine purchase quantity restrictions mirror Federal regulations.
    - Maximum quantity ranges from 3.6 g of base product per day, 9.0 g of base product per 30 days, or 7.5 g of base product per 30 days when sold via mail.
    - Purchaser must be $\geq$ 16 years of age and have a valid, government-issued photo ID.
  - Must be stored behind the counter.
    - If located elsewhere, it must be within 30 feet of the pharmacy or in direct line of sight from the pharmacy counter or sales counter (not necessarily the pharmacy).
  - A record of all transactions must be kept in either an electronic or written logbook.
    - Contents should include the name and quantity of the products sold, purchaser names and addresses, and purchase dates and times.
    - However, sales of a "convenience" package (< 60 mg pseudoephedrine) do not require a logbook.
    - Real-time electronic database tracking of transactions must be reported to a real-time electronic database before completing the sale.

- **Dangerous Drugs Act**
(Texas Health and Safety Code § 483)

  - Dangerous Drugs
    - Any drug/device unsafe for self-medication that might have the following listed:
      - Caution: Federal law prohibits dispensing without prescription.

- Caution: Federal law restricts this drug to use by or on the order of a licensed veterinarian.
- Rx only.
- Any similar legend that complies with Federal law.
- CS I – V or Penalty Groups 1 – 4 of the Texas CS Act are not in this category.
- Possession of a dangerous drug is unlawful unless a pharmacist has delivered it according to a valid prescription or in the usual course of practice.

Emergency Kits
(Texas Pharmacy Act § 562.108; Texas Pharmacy Rules § 291.121)

- Current list of drugs in each kit must be maintained by the provider pharmacy.
- Automated pharmacy systems can be used as emergency kits.
- Drugs used in emergency kits must be in original manufacturer containers or prepackaged in the provider pharmacy and labeled in compliance with BOP regulations.

Closing a Pharmacy
(Texas Pharmacy Rules § 291.5)

- Minimum of 14 days before the pharmacy's permanent closing, the PIC must perform the following:
  - Display a closing notice sign in a clear and visible place in front of the prescription department and at all public entrance doors to the pharmacy containing the closing date and the name, address, and telephone number of the pharmacy acquiring the prescription drug orders, refill information, and patient medication records of the pharmacy.
- DEA must be notified of any CS being transferred to another pharmacy.
- All prescription drug order files, refill information, and patient medication records must be transferred to another licensed pharmacy.
- Within 10 days after closing, the PIC must forward to the BOP a written notice of the closing and include the following:
  - Actual closing date.
  - License issued to the pharmacy.
  - A statement citing that an inventory has been conducted.
  - How the pharmacy's drugs (including CS) were transferred or disposed of.
    - For CS, a notification to the appropriate DEA divisional office explaining that the pharmacy has closed with the pharmacy's DEA registration certificate and all unused DEA order forms (222) with the word VOID written on the face of each order form.
- On the date of closing, the PIC must perform an inventory of prescription drugs (including CS II to CS V), remove all prescription drugs from the pharmacy by returning them to the manufacturer or supplier, sell or give away prescription drugs to a person who is legally entitled to possess drugs (i.e., a hospital or another pharmacy), or destroy the prescription drugs.
- If the pharmacy re-opens, it must apply to the BOP for a new license.
- Emergency closing may occur following fire, destruction, natural disaster, death, property seizure, eviction, bankruptcy, or other emergency circumstances when the PIC cannot provide notification 14 days before the closing.
  - The PIC must comply with the previously described tasks as far in advance of the closing as allowed by the circumstances.
  - If no PIC can do this, the owner must perform these duties.

Destruction of Drugs
(Texas Pharmacy Rules § 303)

- Healthcare facilities or institutions
    - The BOP can destroy dangerous drugs dispensed to patients in healthcare facilities or institutions.
        - Consultant pharmacists can do CS destruction under Federal and DEA regulations.
    - Dangerous drug destruction
        - A written agreement exists between the facility and the consultant pharmacist.
        - The current inventory is complete with accurate documentation of the drug, quantity, and dosage form being destroyed. The signature of the witness(es) and method of destruction are also documented.
            - The method of destruction must render the drugs unfit for human consumption and disposed of according to Federal law.
            - The witness does not need to be a pharmacist or medical professional but could include a commissioned peace officer, an agent of the BOP, an agent of the Texas Health and Human Services Commission (authorized by the BOP to destroy drugs), an agent of the Texas Department of State Health Services (authorized by the BOP to destroy drugs), or any two individuals who are of administrative ranking at the facility.
        - Drugs may be transferred to another institution for destruction that meets the above requirements.
            - Transfer requirements include sealing given drugs in tamper-resistant containers and explicit notation that the drugs are for destruction.
    - The consultant pharmacist must maintain all records required for destruction at the healthcare facility or institution for 2 years from the destruction date.
- Drugs returned to a pharmacy
    - A pharmacist in a pharmacy may accept and destroy dangerous drugs previously dispensed to a patient and returned to a pharmacy by the patient or their agent.
    - This can include CS returned by patients and pharmacy stock CS when permitted by the DEA.

- **Prescriptive Authority**
  (Texas Medical Practice Act § 157.0511; Texas Statutes § 351.358)

    - Mid-level providers (Advanced Practice Nurses (APNs) and Physician Assistants (PAs)) are those who have prescriptive authority dependent on a supervising physician.
        - Cannot prescribe CS IIs
            - Exceptions
                - Patient is in a hospital facility-based practice setting and expects to stay ≥ 24 hours.
                - Patient is in an emergency department and/or will have the prescription filled at the facility's pharmacy only.
                - Patient has a written certification of a terminal illness, has chosen to receive hospice care, and is receiving hospice care by a qualified provider.
        - CS III – V prescribing is permitted.
        - Cannot exceed a 90-day supply (including refills).
        - Children < 2 years old
            - The provider must consult with the delegating physician and note the consultation in the patient's chart.
        - Physicians may delegate prescriptive authority to ≤ 7 PAs or APNs.
            - ≥ 7 delegates are permitted in medically underserved areas or facility-based medical practices in hospital settings.

- Out-of-state mid-level provider prescriptions (not CS) are accepted if they have prescriptive authority in their home state.
- Optometrists
    - Optometrists (with no T or G in their license number) do not have prescriptive authority.
    - Therapeutic optometrists (T in license number) do have limited prescriptive authority.
    - Only topical medications for diagnosing and treating visual defects, abnormal conditions, and diseases of the human visual system.
    - Optometric glaucoma specialists (G in license number) can prescribe like therapeutic optometrists but can also prescribe oral medications used to treat the eye and local tissues.
    - May only prescribe a 3-day supply of any CS III – V drug.

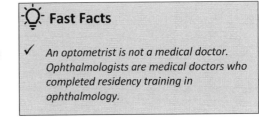

Fast Facts

✓ An optometrist is not a medical doctor. Ophthalmologists are medical doctors who completed residency training in ophthalmology.

- **Prescriptions From Outside State or Country**
(Texas Pharmacy Rules § 291.34)

    - Prescriptions are accepted by providers granted prescriptive authority in any state.
    - Prescriptions and prescription refills from Canada or Mexico can be accepted if they are original, written prescriptions and are NOT CS II – V prescriptions.
    - Prescriptions from any other country are not valid.

- **Pharmacy Complaints**
(Texas Pharmacy Rules §281.21)

    - Patients must be informed of the contact information for the BOP for reporting complaints concerning pharmacy practice.
    - BOP-provided sign must be posted in the pharmacy.
        - If not, a notification must be given with each prescription in no smaller than size 10 font stating, "Complaints concerning the practice of pharmacy may be filed with the Texas State Board of Pharmacy at (current mailing address, internet site address, and telephone number of the Board, and if applicable, a toll-free number for filing complaints)."

CONTROLLED SUBSTANCES (CS)

- **Prescriptions**
  (Texas Pharmacy Rules § 315.3)

  - CS II prescriptions must be written on a Texas Official Prescription Form obtained through the Texas Department of Public Safety OR an electronic prescription that meets the requirements of the Controlled Substances Act.
    - Out-of-state prescriptions are not valid in Texas since official prescription forms are required, and only Texas-registered physicians can order official forms.
      - The exception is if the practitioner is authorized by the other state to prescribe CS IIs, the pharmacy has an approved plan on file with the BOP to allow the activity, and the pharmacy follows this plan for submission of the prescription and reporting requirements.
    - Prescription is valid for only 30 days, except for long-term care facility patients or terminally ill patients (60 days)
  - Each official prescription has preprinted information, including a unique serial number, full name, prescriber's address, and DEA and Department of Public Safety (DPS) registration numbers.
  - When dispensing a CS, the pharmacist must sign, date, and write the prescription number on the preprinted blanks.
    - May only contain one order per prescription form.
    - Multiple CS II prescriptions with a "do not fill before" date or equivalent can be used.
      - The sum of the quantities cannot exceed a 90-day supply.
  - Exceptions to the Texas Official Prescription Form
    - Inpatient medication orders
    - Emergency quantity of CS II upon release from the hospital
    - Life-flight, ambulance crews, or paramedic emergency medical technicians treating patients
    - Prescriptions for inmates in a correctional facility operated by the Texas Department of Criminal Justice
    - Animal hospitals
    - Therapeutic optometrists, specifically administering topical cocaine

- **CS Prescribing Authority of Providers**
  (Texas Medical Practice Act § 157.0511, Texas Statutes § 351.358)

  - Mid-level providers cannot prescribe CS II drugs.
    - Cannot prescribe over a 90-day supply of CS III – V drugs.
  - Therapeutic optometrists may only prescribe a 3-day supply of CS III – V drugs.

- **CS Partial Fills**
  (Texas Pharmacy Rules § 315)
  - CS II Drugs
  - Remaining quantity must be dispensed within 72 hours.
    - After 72 hours, the remaining quantity cannot be dispensed, and the prescriber must be contacted.
  - Pharmacists must note the quantity of medication dispensed initially on the face of the prescription.
  - Exceptions exist for partial filling of CS II drugs for long-term care facility patients and hospice care patients with documented terminal illnesses.

- One of these designations must be recorded in the electronic prescription record, along with the date of partial filling, quantity dispensed, remaining quantity, and dispensing pharmacist's identity.
      - Dispensed quantity may not exceed the original total quantity.
  - CS III through CS V
      - Up to 5 refills in a 6-month-period

- **Records**
  (Texas Pharmacy Rules § 315)

  - CS II records must be separate from all other records of the pharmacy.
  - CS III-V maintained separately or readily retrievable from all other records.

- **Transfers**
  (Texas Pharmacy Rules § 291.34(g))
  - CS III – V can be transferred one time only.
      - If pharmacies share electronic databases, CS III – V can be transferred up to the maximum refills permitted (5).

- **Storage**
  (Texas Pharmacy Rules § 291.17; 291.74; 315)

  - Proper storage of C-II through C-V:
      - The PIC is responsible for taking the required inventories. When inventory is completed, the date and time must be documented along with the signature of the PIC.
          - May be delegated to another person.
      - Class A may store CS II – Vs scattered among other inventory to deter diversion or in a properly locked area.
      - Class C are required to store CS IIs in a locked area (i.e., automated dispensing cabinet, such as Pyxis or Omnicell).
      - Class C must also conduct annual controlled substance inventories on May 1.

- **Prescriptions from Outside Texas or the US**
  (Texas Pharmacy Rules § 291.34)

  - May dispense CS prescriptions from physicians, dentists, podiatrists, and veterinarians who are authorized in their state and have a DEA number.
  - CS II prescriptions by physicians, dentists, podiatrists, and veterinarians may be dispensed if the order is an original written prescription and is dispensed within 30 days of the date written.
  - CS III – V prescriptions by physicians, dentists, podiatrists, and veterinarians may be dispensed if they are not > 6 months from the initial date written and are not refilled > 5 times.
  - However, out-of-state APNs and PAs cannot write prescriptions for any CS.

- **Naloxone**
  (Texas Pharmacy Rules § 295.14)

  - Pharmacists are permitted to dispense naloxone formulations under a standing order, including intramuscular or intranasal naloxone.
  - Pharmacies are permitted to dispense any other items necessary for the administration of naloxone, including syringes, mucosal atomization devices, and other related items.

- – Pharmacists must obtain a certificate of completion of a 1-hour, Texas-accredited course provided by an ACPE-approved provider in coordination with the Texas Pharmacy Association (TPA).
    - – Minimally, training must include when a pharmacist should or should not dispense naloxone under this standing order, how to work with the patient when selecting which dosage form to dispense, and when to administer the naloxone.
  - – Standing order is maintained during the term of the standing order.

- **Medical Marijuana**
  (Texas Occupations Code § 169.002-169.003)

  - – Tetrahydrocannabinol (THC) cannabis can be prescribed under Texas's Compassionate Use Program (CUP) by certified physicians for medical purposes.
    - – Limited to patients with epilepsy, seizure disorder, multiple sclerosis, spasticity, amyotrophic lateral sclerosis, autism, terminal cancer, or an incurable neurodegenerative disease.
    - – Patients must be a permanent resident of Texas.
  - – Patients < 18 may need a legal guardian for consent, but there are technically no age restrictions.

- **Reporting**
  (Texas Pharmacy Rules § 315.15)

  - – Texas Prescription Monitoring Program (PMP)
    - – Applies to all CS II – V drugs dispensed by a pharmacy in Texas or to a Texas resident from a pharmacy located in another state.
    - – Collects and monitors prescription data history.
  - – All Texas-licensed pharmacies are required to report all dispensed CS records to PMP no later than the next business day after the prescription is filled.
  - – Pharmacists and prescribers (other than a veterinarian) must check the patient's PMP history before dispensing or prescribing opioids, benzodiazepines, barbiturates, or carisoprodol.

References

- Texas Board of Pharmacy Rules (https://www.pharmacy.texas.gov/Rules_Pharmacy_Rules.asp)
- Texas Health And Safety Code (https://www.pharmacy.texas.gov/Rules_Other_Pharmacy_Laws_Regs.asp)
- Texas Pharmacy Act (https://www.pharmacy.texas.gov/Rules_Pharmacy_Act.asp)
- Texas Administrative Code (https://www.sos.state.tx.us)
- Texas Medical Practice Act (https://www.tmb.state.tx.us/page/practice-acts)

2024
LIVE IN-PERSON
NAPLEX
RAPID REVIEW

10/10 would recommend to every pharmacy student!
- Amber Gafford

Accelerate your review with us as we cover ALL NABP Topic Areas in just 2 Days!

To get notified about our 2024 In-Person Review, just scan the above QR code and add yourself to our 2024 NAPLEX Contact List.

Need NAPLEX Study Tools?
We have those too!

Join 350+ fellow colleagues and study together!

FREE
NAPLEX
STUDY GROUP

- Ask questions
- Get free fast facts & practice questions from High-Yield faculty
- Stay accountable
- Share study tips
- Don't go it alone!

Join the community today at:
facebook.com/groups/mynaplexstudygroup

Need help with the NAPLEX exam?

High-Yield Med Review's
Study Tools for the NAPLEX

> *"Our comprehensive program and tools were strategically built, using proven strategies, with every student's learning style in mind. You will pass the NAPLEX the first time, we guarantee it."*
>
> — Anthony Busti, MD, PharmD, MSc, FNLA, FAHA

Lectures & Books

- Reflects content tested
- 240+ topics available
- Organized by topic areas
- HD lectures for quality
- Works on all devices
- Monitors your progress

Q-Bank

- 2,000+ practice questions
- Select topic categories
- Teaching points provided
- Performance statistics
- Ability to flag questions
- Peer comparison metrics

Live Reviews

- Live, in-person events
- Live stream events
- Study with your peers
- Taught by expert faculty

Practice Exam

- 150 question exam
- Delivered on computer
- Build test taking skills
- Gain endurance
- Assess your level of preparation

Rapid Review

- Review core concepts quickly.
    - NAPLEX Rapid Review Book
    - NAPLEX Rapid Review Webinar Series
- Final step in comprehensive review

Other Study Tools

- MPJE Exam - Law Review
- Top 300 Drugs Review
- Other tools available :
    - Top 65 Acute Care Drugs
    - Top 50 OTC Drug Review
    - Top 25 Herbals Review
    - Landmark Clinical Trials Reviews

Want to upgrade at a discount?

Need help or a study plan?

We can help!
Contact us for a discount to upgrade to our premium package for the tools you need to prepare and pass.
customerservice@highyieldmedreviews.com

Made in the USA
Columbia, SC
05 December 2023

27814184R00083